Code Happy

Application development with the Laravel PHP Framework for beginners.

Copyright 2012 Dayle Rees.

Published: 07 July 2012.

ISBN: 978-1-4717-7749-3

Contents

Acknowledgements

First of all I would like to thank my girlfriend Emma, for not only putting up with all my nerdy ventures, but also for taking the amazing red panda shot for the book's cover! Love you Emma!

Taylor Otwell, I love you too man, but in a totally manly way. Thanks for making a framework that's a real pleasure to use, makes our code read like poetry, and for putting so much time and passion into it's development.

Eric Barnes, Phill Sparks, Shawn McCool, Jason Lewis, Ian Landsman, thanks for all the support with the framework, and for allowing me to be part of a project with so much potential.

Thanks to my parents, who have been supportive no matter how nerdy I have become!

To all my blog readers who took interest in my tutorials, thanks! Without you I would never have had the confidence to write a book.

Errata

Although I have taken every care to ensure that the book is error-free, sometimes tired eyes will proof read badly, and errors will slip through the radar. If you do happen to encounter an error in the book, be it a spelling mistake or an error within a code block, I would be grateful if you could alert me to its presence by emailing me at me@daylerees.com[1] including the chapter and location of the error.

Errors will be fixed as they are discovered, and fixes will be released within future editions of the book.

---

[1]mailto:me@daylerees.com

Feedback

Likewise you can send any feedback you may have about the content of the book or otherwise by sending an email to me@daylerees.com[2]. I will endeavour to reply to all mail that I receive about the book.

[2]mailto:me@daylerees.com

Introduction

Hi there! I'm Dayle Rees, and I'm going to be taking you on a magical journey into the world of Laravel! Okay on second thoughts that sounds really cheesy. You see this is my first book, so I am gonna be a little rusty at all the posh literary stuff. So if you like straight talking, and being "spoken" to like a real human being then boy are you in for a treat!

You might be asking yourselves "So why should I trust this guy to teach me Laravel? He isn't even an experienced author!"

Well what I lack in experience, I make up for in enthusiasm. I am a huge fan of web development, and the tools and tricks that save us time or make our jobs a lot easier. Laravel fills both of those requirements, and is one of the most useful pieces of software I have ever discovered. In fact my enthusiasm and passion for the framework, that can only be rivalled by the framework author himself has led to me being included as a member of the Laravel core team and "Council" as we like to call it, sounds fancier right?

Being on the Laravel Core team grants me certain privileges such as being notified of new ideas and planned additions to the framework, and by contributing to the framework I am constantly in touch with its forever improving code base. This puts me in a great position to keep the book up to date, which I intend to do with every future release of the framework.

Although I despise going off-topic, it seems compulsory to have a short paragraph about the author within books of this kind, so let's keep it short and sweet. I live on the coast of Wales (that's a country on the side of England for you Americans) and I work for a large public sector organisation in Aberystwyth. In my spare time I am highly involved with the Laravel framework. Oh and as I said before, I don't claim to be a literary genius, let's be honest my writing is gonna suck, it's not gonna be all fancy like those other coding books. I will be 'talking' to you like a real person, you might actually talk back too, we will see. Hopefully my passion for Laravel will make up for my common English (to be fair, I am a Welshman). You don't need to know anything more about me though, let's switch our focus to Laravel.

Laravel is a breath of fresh air in the world of PHP. The PHP programming language is generally quite renowned for its ugly function names, and while we PHP developers have learned to love it, the syntax can be a little ugly compared to some modern Japanese languages. Hi Ruby!

Fortunately Laravel changes this, in fact.. I believe that the Laravel syntax (which granted builds on PHP's own) is so expressive and neat that I find it much easier to read than Ruby. It's not too compact, and while it won't read like an English sentence, it will read like poetry that can only be seen by the eyes of a programmer.

But Dayle..

You say, suddenly worried that your money could have been better spent on some mind numbing fun juice.

Laravel is a framework, not a language!

It's true, you got me. Laravel may not be a language, but it doesn't need to be. We love PHP, come on, let's be honest, we put up with its ugliness, we enjoy typing all those brackets and semi-colons. Laravel simply adds the short-cuts, or a code disguise on top to make the experience so much sweeter.

I think that the pleasure of working from the framework is brought on by its expressive methods which are consistent throughout the framework. `Str::upper()` Try to tell me you don't know what this does, try to tell me it doesn't make sense.

I can't.

Yep, I thought so. Well I could jabber on all day about everything that makes Laravel wonderful. Let's see, there's Eloquent, the best ORM I have ever seen. It was what first brought me to the framework.

The option of using closures to route, but only if you want to. I think they look great!

Not having to load libraries before using them, yes.. you heard me right. You will see this in action later.

No there are far too many wonderful features to explain here, I think it would be best if we dived in and started learning, after all.. if you spent your money on this instead of mind numbing juice, you must already have had your interests peaked by the framework right? Onwards!

1 Getting Started

Laravel[1] is a PHP 5.3 web application framework written by Taylor Otwell[2]. It was written with PHP 5.3 features in mind. The combination of these features and its very expressive syntax has led to the framework gaining in popularity.

In this book we will be exploring Laravel from the ground up starting with its installation, which I am sure you will agree is a breeze.

In order to use any PHP Framework (not just Laravel) you will need to have a PHP enabled web server, I would recommend installing a web server on your local development machine, to allow you to test your work without needing to upload your files each time you make a change.

This chapter makes the following assumptions:

- You have a working Apache-based web server with PHP5.3+.
- You are familiar with the server's file system, and how to move / copy files.
- You have access to modify Apache configuration files.

If you are using a different web server, you will be able to find many articles on-line on how to accomplish the tasks found below for your server.

First we will need a copy of the framework's source code, simply head over to Laravel.com[3] and hit the big orange download button. For added security, I would recommend extracting the contents of the package to somewhere other than your web root. Make a mental note of where you extracted the source to (or find a sticky note!).

We now have two options to allow the framework to execute as expected, I would advise trying the first method as it is the "real" way of installing the framework and will allow us to specify a more thorough configuration. However I find the second method much quicker when working with many projects on a development server.

1.1 Method 1 Create a new VirtualHost

We will need to create a new Apache configuration file. On most standard installations creating a `myproject.conf` file in the Apache `conf.d` directory will include it by default, please see the documentation for your current set-up for more information.

Inside our new configuration file, paste or type the following VirtualHost declaration:

```
1  <VirtualHost 127.0.0.2>
2          DocumentRoot "/path/to/laravel/project/public"
3          ServerName myproject
```

---

[1] http://laravel.com
[2] https://twitter.com/#!/taylorotwell
[3] http://laravel.com

```
4        <Directory "/path/to/laravel/project/public">
5                Options Indexes FollowSymLinks MultiViews
6                AllowOverride all
7        </Directory>
8   </VirtualHost>
```

We must update the IP address to one which is not currently in use. (Best not to use 127.0.0.1, this is your loop-back address, and you may have something else using it.) Change the two paths to point to your Laravel source package's public directory. Now restart your web server.

Next we will create a new local DNS entry to point a project name to your VirtualHost. First open the hosts file normally found at c:\windows\system32\drivers\etc\hosts on a Windows machine or /etc/hosts on unix-based operating systems.

Add the following line using the IP address and server name you used in your VirtualHost declaration:

```
1   127.0.0.2              myproject
```

You should now be able to navigate to http://myproject with your web browser to see the Laravel welcome page.

1.2 Method 2 Symbolic link the public directory.

If you are familiar with using symbolic links on a unix-based system, this method will prove rather simple.

Inside the extracted Laravel source code (you remember where you put it, right?) you will find a sub directory called 'public'. This directory contains the Laravel bootstrap file and all public assets. We will be symbolic linking this directory to your public web root (possibly /var/www/html/).

To create the symbolic link simply execute the following command in your terminal of choice, replacing the paths where necessary.

```
1   ln -s /path/to/laravel/public/directory /path/to/web/root/subdirectory
```

For example :

```
1   ln -s /home/dayle/laravel/myapp/public /var/www/html/myapp
```

Note: You could also symbolic link the public directory directly to your web root, but I prefer using a subdirectory so I can work on several projects.

You should now be able to navigate to http://localhost/myapp with your web browser to see the Laravel welcome page.

1.3 Getting back on track..

At this point you should now be able to see your Laravel welcome page, if so..

Congratulations! You have a brand new Laravel project, you are now ready to get coding!

In the next chapter we will be covering the Laravel project structure, and providing an explanation of each of the important files and directories.

If you happen to find any of the topics covered in this book confusing, the following links can be used to find the help and support you need, or simply post a new comment on DayleRees.com[4].

- Laravel Website[5]

- Laravel Docs[6]

- Laravel API[7]

- Laravel Forums[8]

Why not come and join our ever expanding community by using an IRC client to connect to `irc.freenode.net:6667` and joining the `#laravel` channel!

---

[4]http://daylerees.com
[5]http://laravel.com
[6]http://laravel.com/docs
[7]http://laravel.com/api
[8]http://forums.laravel.com

2 Project Structure

Laravel's source package contains a number of different directories. Let's take a look at the project structure to gain a greater understanding of how things work. I may use some terms to describe various features of Laravel that could be confusing if you are just starting out, if so, bear with me as we will cover each feature in more detail in a later chapter.

2.1 Root Directory Structure

Lets take a quick look at the top-level file and directory structure :

```
1  /application
2  /bundles
3  /laravel
4  /public
5  /storage
6  /vendor
7  /artisan [file]
8  /paths.php [file]
```

Now lets take a closer look at each item :

/application

This is where the majority of the code for your application will live. It contains your routing, data models and views. You will be spending most of your time here!

/bundles

Bundles are Laravel applications. They can be used to separate aspects of your application, or can be released / downloaded to share common code[1]. By installing new bundles with artisan, you can extend the functionality of Laravel to suit your needs.

Interestingly, the /application **directory is also a bundle known as the** DEFAULT_BUNDLE, **this means that anything you use in** /application **you can also use in your bundles!**

/laravel

This is where the framework's core files live. These are the files it needs to execute a request. You will rarely have to interact with this directory, but it can sometimes be useful to browse the source to see how a Class or Method works. Alternatively you could check the Laravel API[2].

/public

This is the directory that you must point your web server to. It contains the bootstrap file index.php which starts the Laravel framework and the routing process. The public directory can also be used to hold any publicly accessible assets such as CSS, Javascript files and images.

---

[1]http://bundles.laravel.com/
[2]http://laravel.com/api

The laravel subdirectory also contains the files needed to render the off-line documentation correctly.

/storage

The storage directory is used as file store for services that use the file system as a driver, for example Sessions, or the Cache class. This directory must be writeable by the web server. You will not need to interact with this directory to build a Laravel application.

/vendor

The vendor directory contains code used by Laravel, but wasn't written by the framework's author or contributors. The directory contains open source software, or parts of software that contribute to Laravel's features.

/artisan [file]

Artisan is Laravel's Command Line Interface. It allows you to perform numerous tasks[3] on the command line. You can even create your own tasks! To run Artisan simply type:

```
1   php artisan
```

/paths.php [file]

This file is used by the framework to determine paths to the important directories mentioned above, and to provide a short-cut for retrieving them (using path()). You should not need to edit this file.

2.2 Application Directory Structure

As mentioned above, /application is where all the fun happens, so let's have a look at the structure of the /application directory.

```
1   /config
2   /controllers
3   /language
4   /libraries
5   /migrations
6   /models
7   /tasks
8   /tests
9   /views
10  /bundles.php [file]
11  /routes.php [file]
12  /start.php [file]
```

---

[3]http://laravel.com/docs/artisan/commands

And now a closer look at each one.

/config

The config directory contains a number of configuration files for changing various aspects of the framework. No configuration needs to be set at install for the framework to work 'out of the box'. Most of the configuration files return key-value PHP arrays of options, sometimes key-closure pairs that allow a great deal of freedom to modify the inner working of some of Laravel's core classes.

/controllers

Laravel provides two methods for routing, using `controllers` and using `routes` to closures. This directory contains the Controller classes that are used to provide basic logic, interact with data models, and load view files for your application. Controllers were added to the framework at a later date to provide familiar ground for users migrating from other frameworks. Although they were added as an afterthought, due to Laravel's powerful routing system, they allow you to perform any action which can be performed using `routes` to closures.

/language

In this directory, PHP files containing arrays of strings exist to enable easy localization of applications built using Laravel. By default the directory contains string files for pagination and form validation in the English language.

/libraries

The libraries directory can be used to 'drop in' single class PHP Libraries to provide extra functionality for your application. For larger Libraries it is recommended that you create a Bundle instead. The libraries directory is added to the Autoloader at startup from the start.php file.

/migrations

The migrations directory contains PHP classes which allow Laravel to update the Schema of your current database, or populate it with values while keeping all versions of the application in sync. Migration files must not be created manually, as their file name contains a timestamp. Instead use the Artisan CLI interface command `php artisan migrate:make <migration_name>` to create a new Migration.

/models

Models are classes that represent your project's data. Normally this would mean integrating with a form of database, or other data source. Laravel provides three methods for interacting with common database platforms, including a query builder named 'Fluent'[4], which allows you to create SQL queries by chaining PHP methods. You could also use the Eloquent ORM to represent your tables as PHP Objects, or use the plain old raw SQL queries that you're used to. Fluent and Eloquent both use a similar syntax, making their adoption a smooth transition.

Files in the models directory are auto-loaded automatically from `start.php`.

/tasks

---

[4]http://laravel.com/docs/database/fluent

By creating classes in the tasks directory, you are able to add your own custom tasks to the Laravel Artisan command line interface. Tasks are represented by classes and methods.

/tests

The tests directory provides a location for you to keep your application unit tests. If you are using PHPUnit, you can execute all tests at once using the Laravel Artisan PHP command line interface.

/views

The views directory contains your HTML template files to be used by controllers or routes, although please use a .php extension for files in this directory. You can alternatively use a .blade.php extension to enable parsing with the Blade templating library which will be explained in a later chapter.

/bundles.php [file]

To enable a bundle, simply add it to the array in bundles.php. You can also use a key-value, name-array pair to define extra options for the bundle.

/routes.php [file]

The routes file contains the methods which enable routes to be mapped to their appropriate outcome with Laravel. This topic will be explained more thoroughly in upcoming chapters. This file also contains declarations for several events including error pages, and can be used to define view composers or route filters.

/start.php [file]

The start.php contains start-up routines for the /application bundle, such as auto-loading directories, loading configuration files, and other wonderful useful stuff! Feel free to append to this file.

In the next chapter we will be cover routing using controllers.

3 Using Controllers

In this chapter we will be creating a simple multi page website to demonstrate the workings of Laravel's routing system, without delving into anything too complicated.

As I mentioned in the previous chapter, there are two options available to route web requests to your code, Controllers and Routes. In this chapter we will be using Controllers since anyone joining us from other frameworks will be more familiar with them.

3.1 Routing Controllers

So let's start by taking a look at a Controller :

```php
<?php

// application/controllers/account.php
class Account_Controller extends Base_Controller
{

    public function action_index()
    {
        echo "This is the profile page.";
    }

    public function action_login()
    {
        echo "This is the login form.";
    }

    public function action_logout()
    {
        echo "This is the logout action.";
    }

}
```

A Controller is a PHP Class that represents a section of your website, or web application. Its Methods or 'Actions' represent an individual page, or an end-point of a HTTP request.

In the above example our Account Controller represents our users section of the web site, a profile page, a login page, and a logout page. Note that the Controller names are appended with _Controller and that action names are prefixed with action_. Controllers must extend the Base_Controller, Controller or another Controller class.

Our controller is created in the application/controllers directory as a lower-case file matching the controller name. The Controller above would be saved at :

```
1   /application/controllers/account.php
```

Before we can use our Controller we will need to register it in /application/routes.php. Let's add the following line :

```
1   <?php
2
3   // application/routes.php .
4   Route::controller('account');
```

If our controller is in a sub-directory of the controllers directory simply use periods (.) to separate the directories like so :

```
1   <?php
2
3   // application/routes.php
4   Route::controller('in.a.sub.directory.account');
```

If our controller exists in a bundle, simply prefix with the bundle name and a double colon :

```
1   <?php
2
3   // application/routes.php
4   Route::controller('mybundle::account');
```

Now if we visit:

```
1   http://myproject/account/login
```

we see This is the login form.. This is because now that our Controller has been mapped in the Route class, the first segment (between the slashes) of the URL specifies the controller, and the second segment (yes, again between the slashes) specifies the action.

In simple terms /account/login is mapped to Account_Controller->action_login() and the result of our method is displayed.

Now let's try visiting /account instead :

```
1   This is the profile page.
```

Why does this happen? The index action is a special action which is called when no action is specified in the URI, therefore the above page could also be "called" with the following URI :

```
1   /account/index
```

3.2 Passing Parameters

This simple routing is interesting, but it doesn't offer us anything that a simple PHP website could not.

Let's try something a little more dynamic. By adding parameters to our controller actions we can pass extra data as segments to the URL. Let's add a welcome action to our controller :

```php
1   <?php
2
3   // application/controllers/account
4   public function action_welcome($name, $place)
5   {
6           echo "Welcome to {$place}, {$name}!";
7   }
```

Here our action parameters are method parameters, so the above code should seem familiar. Let's try visiting the route /account/welcome/Dayle/Wales..

```
1   Welcome to Wales, Dayle!
```

Parameters can be used to pass resource identifiers to enable CRUD actions on data, or anything you can think of! As you can see, they offer a great deal of flexibility to our actions.

Note : You can assign values to your action parameters to make them optional in the URL.

3.3 Using Views

Echoing out source from our Controllers yields a result, but it's not an elegant solution. If you are interested in learning Laravel then elegant solutions may well have been what brought you here. The nature of MVC suggests that we separate our visual layer from the application's logic. This is where the 'Views' portion of the pattern comes into play.

With Laravel, views could not not be simpler. Simply add HTML templates to your /application/views/ directory with a lower-case file name, and a .php extension. For example :

```
1   /application/views/welcome.php
```

With the contents :

```
1   <h1>Holla!</h1>
2   <p>This is the welcome action of the account controller.</p>
```

Now we need to return the View from our welcome action. Laravel has a beautiful expressive way of doing this, let's take a look :

```php
1   <?php
2
3   // application/controllers/account.php
4   public function action_welcome($name, $place)
5   {
6           return View::make('welcome');
7   }
```

The more nerdy types among my readers will have realized that the statement is telling Laravel to create (make) a View object from the file `application/views/welcome.php` (extension not needed here) and return it as the result of the welcome action.

You will also notice that the `make()` method looks in the `application/views` directory for its views. If you would like to specify an absolute path to a view file simply use the `path:` prefix, for example `path: /path/to/my/view.php`.

Now if we visit `/account/welcome/Dayle/Wales` we will be greeted with the web page which we defined in our View file.

Note that you can also use the same sub-directory and bundle prefixes that we previously used with controllers, to refer to Views.

I know what you're thinking, now our welcome message isn't very dynamic at all? Let's see if we can fix this. Let's pass our action parameters to the View. We can do this using the `with()` method and we can see Laravel's elegant method chaining in action, here we go!

```php
1   <?php
2
3   // application/controllers/account.php
4   public function action_welcome($name, $place)
5   {
6           return View::make('welcome')
7                   ->with('name', $name)
8                   ->with('place', $place);
9   }
```

Using the `with()` method we can pass any value (or object) to the View and give it a 'nickname' for accessing it from the view. We have used the same nicknames as our parameter names in this example, but you can call them anything you want!

Now let's use this data in our view :

```php
1   <h1>Holla!</h1>
2   <p>Welcome to <?php echo $place; ?>, <?php echo $name; ?>!</p>
```

Now our action works as it did before, only better formatted with neater source code separating all logic from our visual layer.

Instead of using several `with()` methods, you can pass an array as a second parameter to `make()` with key-value pairs. This can save space but has the same result, here is an example.

```php
1   <?php
2
3   // application/controllers/account.php
4   public function action_welcome($name, $place)
5   {
6           $data = array(
7                   'name'              => $name,
8                   'place' => $place
9           );
10
11           return View::make('welcome', $data);
12  }
```

Note : I like to call my view array $data, **but you can call it whatever you want!**

In a later chapter we will cover Views in more detail, including Blade templating, nested views and other advanced templating options.

3.4 RESTful Controllers

RESTful web applications respond to meaningful HTTP verbs with appropriate data. They are very useful when building public API's for your applications.

With Laravel you can have your controller actions respond to individual HTTP verbs using RESTful controller actions, let's see this in action.

```php
1   <?php
2
3   // application/controllers/home.php
4   class Home_Controller extends Base_Controller
5   {
6       public $restful = true;
7
8       public function get_index()
9       {
10          //
11      }
12
13      public function post_index()
14      {
15          //
16      }
17
18  }
```

Simply add a boolean public class attribute named $restful and set it to true, then prefix your actions with the HTTP verb to respond to rather than action_.

Common HTTP verbs are GET, POST, PUT and DELETE.

3.5 The Base_Controller

You can edit the Base_Controller, and extend it with your other Controllers to provide global functionality across all of your controllers. Add a default action index or class values, anything you want!

The Base_Controller can be found in /application/controllers/base.php.

If you do not wish to use a Base_Controller, simply have your controllers extend the 'Controller' class instead.

3.6 Advanced Routing

Now we are able to map our controllers and actions to URI's in the format /controller/action/param/param/... which is great, but we shouldn't be restricted to using only this format. Let's see if we can break out of the mold. Earlier we placed a controller declaration in routes.php but now let's replace it with the following code.

```
1  <?php
2
3  //application/routes.php
4  Route::get('superwelcome/(:any)/(:any)', 'account@welcome');
```

Here we are saying, let's send all web requests with the GET HTTP verb, and the address /superwelcome/(:any)/(:any) to the welcome action of the account controller.

The (:any) segments are place-holders for our parameters, and will be passed in the order that they are provided. Using (:num) will match only numbers, and using (:any?) will create an optional segment.

So now a visit to /superwelcome/Dayle/Wales will show our lovely view page!

The advantage of defining routes is that we can have our URLs in whatever order we like, in whatever format we like. For example we could also have..

```
1  <?php
2
3  //application/routes.php
4  Route::get('superwelcome/(:any)/(:any)', 'account@welcome');
5  Route::get('welcome/(:any)/to/(:any)', 'account@welcome');
```

Now we have two different routes, with the same result page.

It is worth noting that Routes that are defined "higher up" in the routes.php file are given a higher priority. With the following example..

```php
1   <?php
2
3   // application/routes.php
4   Route::get('(:any)/(:any)', 'account@welcome');
5   Route::get('welcome/(:any)/to/(:any)', 'account@welcome');
```

..the second route would never be triggered because the (:any) in the first route would respond to the welcome in the second route. This is a common mistake when starting out with Laravel. Be sure to keep an eye on the priority of your routes!

We will be covering routing in more depth in the next chapter which will also cover routing with closures instead of controllers.

4 Routes With Closures

In this chapter we will be using ***Routes with Closures*** instead of ***Controllers with Actions***. If you have not yet read the previous chapter on the topic of using controllers then I would suggest starting there since we will be building on what we have already learned in this chapter.

Routes allow us to map our framework URLs to closures, which is a very clean way of containing our logic without all of the 'class fluff'. Closures are anonymous functions (function() {}), they can be assigned to and treated like any other variable. For more information on Closures, check out the PHP API article[1].

4.1 Closures

Lets have a look at a route that routes to a closure.

```php
<?php

// application/routes.php
Route::get('/', function()
{
        return View::make('home.index');
});
```

In this example we are responding to requests to the root of the web application that use the HTTP verb GET with a closure that simply returns a view object. The output is the default welcome page.

Please note that you only need the root slash for the root page, all other routes omit it, for example..

```php
<?php

// application/routes.php
Route::get('account/profile', function()
{
        return View::make('account.profile');
});
```

Routes are RESTful by nature, but you can use Route::any() to respond to any HTTP verb. Here are your options:

---

[1]http://php.net/manual/en/functions.anonymous.php

```php
1   <?php
2
3   // application/routes.php
4   Route::get();
5   Route::post();
6   Route::put();
7   Route::delete();
8   Route::any();
```

To pass parameters to your closures simply add the usual view place-holders to the URI, and define parameters in your closure. They will be matched in the order from left to right, for example..

```php
1   <?php
2
3   // application/routes.php
4   Route::get('user/(:any)/task/(:num)', function($username, $task_number)
5   {
6           // $username will be replaced by the value of (:any)
7           // $task_number will be replaced by the integer in place of (:num)
8
9           $data = array(
10                  'username'          => $username,
11                  'task'                  => $task_number
12          );
13
14          return View::make('tasks.for_user', $data);
15  });
```

Available placeholders are:

Placeholder	Explanation
(:any)	Match any alpha-numeric string
(:num)	Match any whole number.
(:any?)	Optional parameter.

4.2 Redirects and Named Routes

It would be kinda silly to look at named routes before seeing a method that uses them wouldn't it? Let's have a look at the Redirect class, it can be used to Redirect to another route. It can be used in a similar fashion to returning a view.

```php
1   <?php
2
```

```
3   // application/routes.php
4   Route::get('/', function()
5   {
6           return Redirect::to('account/profile');
7   });
```

Lovely! Couldn't be simpler, wait no, it could, and is! Lets take a look at a named route :

```
1   <?php
2
3   Route::get('account/profile', array('as' => 'profile', 'do' => function()
4   {
5           return View::make('account/profile');
6   }));
```

Instead of passing a Closure as the second parameter, we now pass an array with the key 'do' pointing to the closure. This allows us to add all kind of extra information to the route.

The 'as' key, assigns a nickname to our route, this is what named routing is all about. Let's see how it can be used to improve the Redirect:: from before.

```
1   <?php
2
3   Route::get('/', function()
4   {
5           return Redirect::to_route('profile');
6   });
```

There, now we have that nasty URI out of our code, very pretty. All of the classes or helpers which refer to routes have a similar method to route to a named route. This can really clean up your code, and makes it read like a book. Also, if you later decide to change the URI for a certain page, you will not have to go back and change all of your links and redirects!

4.3 Filters

Ok ok... I said I was going to be explaining Routes in this one, but I honestly can't think of a better place to cover Filters, and they are related, so here we go.

Filters are exactly as they sound, they are code or tests that can be performed 'before' or 'after' a route, and other key events within the framework. Laravel has four special route filters that are defined by default in application/routes.php. Let's take a look at them.

```
1   <?php
2
3   Route::filter('before', function()
```

```
4  {
5          // Do stuff before every request to your application...
6  });
7
8  Route::filter('after', function($response)
9  {
10          // Do stuff after every request to your application...
11  });
12
13  Route::filter('csrf', function()
14  {
15          if (Request::forged()) return Response::error('500');
16  });
17
18  Route::filter('auth', function()
19  {
20          if (Auth::guest()) return Redirect::to('login');
21  });
```

The first two routes execute the encapsulated closure before and after every request (or route / action) to your application. What you do within the enclosure is entirely up to you. Start libraries, provide data to 'something', your own creativity is your only limitation. They are special filters in that they do not need to be assigned to individual routes.

The 'csrf' filter is used to prevent 'cross-site-request-forgery[2]' and can be applied to routes which are the result of an AJAX call for extra security.

The 'auth' filter can be applied to any route to prevent access unless a user is currently 'logged in' using Laravel's authentication system.

To apply 'csrf' or 'auth' filters to your Routes, simply add a new array entry to the second parameter like so:

```
1  <?php
2
3  Route::get('/', array('as' => 'profile', 'before' => 'auth', 'do' => functi\
4  on()
5  {
6          return View::make('account/profile');
7  }));
```

The key for the array can be either 'before' to run the filter before your route, or 'after' to run it after. Multiple filters can be applied by separating their names with a | (pipe) for example auth|csrf.

As of Laravel 3.1, if you would like to add a filter to a number of requests whose URIs match a specific pattern, use the following line :

---

[2]http://en.wikipedia.org/wiki/Cross-site_request_forgery

```php
1   <?php
2
3   Route::filter('pattern: admin/*', 'auth');
```

This will apply the 'auth' filter to all route URIs that start with admin/.

4.4 Route Groups

You may want to apply a number of settings across a range of routes. You can do this easily using the route grouping option, take a look..

```php
1   <?php
2
3   Route::group(array('before' => 'auth'), function()
4   {
5           Route::get('panel', function()
6           {
7                   // do stuff
8           });
9
10          Route::get('dashboard', function()
11          {
12                  // do stuff
13          });
14  });
```

Now both the panel and dashboard routes are protected by the 'auth' filter.

Although routing can be very simple, routes can also be as complex as you need them to be. Use route groups to avoid duplicating common rules across many routes and keep your code DRY. (Don't repeat yourself!)

The next chapter will cover the creation of links, so that we can move from one routes page to the next. Hopefully you will already know how to move from one book page to the next.

5 Links and URLs

Our application might get a little boring if we only have one page, and I'm sure the user would get peeved quite quickly if they had to type out the full URI each time to switch pages. Fortunately, hyper-links are here to save the day.

If you haven't been living under a rock for the past couple of decades you will already know what hyper-links are and I won't bore you with the technical explanation. Before we have a look at links let's take a look at how Laravel handles its URLs.

5.1 Retrieving URLs

First let's take a look at a problem. You see frameworks have very unique URL structures. Some may have an index.php in them, some installations won't. Others will have complex routes. In most cases using a relative URL like you would on another website would lead to trouble in the long run. If you chose to provide full URL's to everything and later decided to move the application to a different domain, you might find yourself abusing the find and replace function of your favourite editor.

Why not let Laravel do all the hard work? Laravel knows the full URL to your application. It knows whether or not you are using URL rewriting. It knows about your routes. It even knows what you keep in that box under your bed.. Let's take advantage of this information by using the URL class to generate some site URLs.

Let's start by finding the URL to the root of our website. We can use the base() method for this.

```php
1   <?php
2
3   echo URL::base();
4   // http://myproject
```

Great! Now we have the full URL to our site, with or without the index.php on the end. It all depends on your current set-up. What about the current URL, the one that is being routed at the moment, can we get that? You betcha! Simply use the current() method.

```php
1   <?php
2
3   echo URL::current();
4   // http://myproject/this/page
```

By default Laravel will strip off the query string if one is appended to the URL. If we want to retrieve the current URL along with the query string, we can use the full() method instead.

```php
1   <?php
2
3   echo URL::full();
4   // http://myproject/this/page?thing=stuff
```

Knowing our base URL and current URL can be handy, but it would be more useful if we could get the URL to other routes or pages, then we could create links.

To generate a URL to a route, we use the to() method, and hand it the route that we are trying to retrieve. This is much easier than specifying the full path, for example..

```php
<?php

echo URL::to('my/route');
// http://myproject/my/route
```

If we want to link to this page securely via the HTTPS protocol we can use the method to_-secure() instead.

```php
<?php

echo URL::to_secure('my/route');
// https://myproject/my/route
```

Do you remember being taught about named routes in the routing chapter? Of course you do! Here's an example of one again..

```php
<?php

Route::get('login', array('as' => 'login', 'do' => function() {
        // some code
}));
```

Here we have a route that we have named 'login' using the 'as' array key. Well I told you that it would be useful later, and now is the time for named routes to shine. Let's make a link to our named 'login' route..

```php
<?php

echo URL::to_route('login');
// http://myproject/login
```

Woah! Very clean and expressive I think you will agree. What if we need to supply parameters to our route? Simple, just pass an array of parameters as a second parameter to the to_route() method. Let's imagine for a second that our login route looks more like this...

```php
<?php

Route::get('my/(:any)/login/(:any)/page')..
```

It's a terrible route, please don't use ugly URL's like this one, but it will help to illustrate a point. You see, if you pass parameters to the `to_route()` method, Laravel will automatically work out which order they should appear in the URL and return the full URL with the parameters in the right place. Neat!

```php
<?php

echo URL::to_route('login', array(5, 7));
```

The above method would give us..

```
http://myproject/my/5/login/7/page
```

Great! Now our routes will look squeaky clean.. as long as we don't create routes as complicated as that one. Also if we decide to change the URI for our route at a later date, we won't need to update all of our links!

So that's routes cleared up, but we shouldn't forget controllers. No one likes to be left out. Fortunately there's a nice and clean way to create a link to a controller action. Simply use the `to_action()` method, for example..

```php
<?php

echo URL::to_action('dashboard@home');
// http://myproject/dashboard/home
```

Just pass the controller name and action, separated by an @ (at) symbol. Once again you can pass an array of extra parameters as a second parameter to the `to_action()` method if you need to.

If we are dealing with assets, a CSS style-sheet for example, rather than routes pages we will need a very different URL. We can't use `URL::to()` because that might put an `index.php` in the URL or resolve it to one of our routes.

Instead we can use the `to_asset()` method to generate a correct link. Simply pass the application relative path to our style-sheet and Laravel will take care of the rest.

```php
<?php

echo URL::to_asset('css/style.css');
```

This line will give us..

```
http://myproject/css/style.css
```

These methods are already very handy, but Laravel takes this a step further by providing shorter `helper` methods which look great when used in our views. Here is a list of these helpers, and their longer alternatives.

Helper	Method
url()	URL::to()
asset()	URL::to_asset()
route()	URL::to_route()
action()	URL::to_action()

5.2 Generating Links

Now that we can retrieve our site URLs, the next logical step would be to use them to create hyper-links. Now I know what you're thinking, we can do it like this..

```
1  <a href="<?php echo URL::to('my/page'); ?>">My Page</a>
```

Sure that would work, but it's a little ugly. In Laravel if something is a little ugly, there is always a better way of handling it. Links are no exception.

Why don't we use the HTML class to generate a link? After all, that's what the HTML class is for. It is used to generate all kinds of HTML tags.

```
1  <?php echo HTML::link('my/page', 'My Page'); ?>
```

That looks a lot better! Let's see the result.

```
1  <a href="http://myproject/my/page">My Page</a>
```

If you are an SEO ninja, and cannot stand to see a link without a title attribute, simply pass an extra array.

```
1  <?php echo HTML::link('my/page', 'My Page', array('title' => 'My page!')); \
2  ?>
```

Which gives..

```
1  <a href="http://myproject/my/page" title="My page!">My Page</a>
```

One of the great features of Laravel is how consistent its method naming is. Many of the HTML::link methods follow a similar naming pattern as the URL::to methods, which makes them easy to remember. Let's take a look at how we can link to a secure page (via HTTPS).

```
1  <?php
2
3  HTML::link_to_secure('my/page', 'My Page');
4  // <a href="https://myproject/my/page">My Page</a>
```

We can also use `link_to_route` to create a link to a named route just like we did with the URL library.

```php
<?php

HTML::link_to_route('login', 'Login!');
// <a href="http://myproject/login/page">Login!</a>
```

Once again we can use the `link_to_action()` method to link to a controller-action pair, for example..

```php
<?php

HTML::link_to_action('account@login', 'Login!');
// <a href="http://myproject/account/login">Login!</a>
```

Laravel even gives us a method of easily creating 'mailto' links from an email address. Let's take a look.

```php
<?php

HTML::mailto('me@daylerees.com', 'Mail me!');
// <a href="mailto:me@daylerees.com">Mail me!</a>
```

Nice and clean!

Now that you know how to create URL's and links, your applications will start to grow in size, covering many routes until they consume our planet and take over the unive...

Your applications will be a lot more interesting!

6 Forms

Forms are an important part of any web-based application. They help control the flow of the application which allows us to receive input from our users and make decisions that affect the functionality of our applications. They are also my least favourite thing in the world to write.

Fortunately for me (and you), Laravel's form class takes care of a lot of the hard work for us by providing useful methods for generating common form elements. Let's use the form class to create a simple web form in one of our views.

6.1 Creating Forms

```php
1   // form.php
2   <?php echo Form::open('my/route'); ?>
3
4       <!-- username field -->
5       <?php echo Form::label('username', 'Username'); ?>
6       <?php echo Form::text('username'); ?>
7
8       <!-- password field -->
9       <?php echo Form::label('password', 'Password'); ?>
10      <?php echo Form::password('password'); ?>
11
12      <!-- login button -->
13      <?php echo Form::submit('Login');
14
15  <?php echo Form::close(); ?>
```

Take a moment, stare at the form source, you have never seen a form so clean. Say it out loud to yourself, go on.. I will wait.

I have never seen a form so clean.

You are right, it's beautiful. Let's have a look at the generated source to make sure I'm not just teaching you wrong, you know, for fun?

```html
1   <form method="POST" action="http://mysite/my/route" accept-charset="UTF-8">
2
3       <!-- username field -->
4       <label for="username">Username</label>
5       <input type="text" name="username" id="username">
6
7       <!-- password field -->
8       <label for="password">Password</label>
```

```
9        <input type="password" name="password" id="password">
10
11       <!-- login button -->
12       <input type="submit" value="Login">
13
14   </form>
```

Great, it worked! I mean of course it did! Let's go over the form line by line to see how it works. On our first line we have the `Form::open()` method which creates a form open tag for us.

```
1    <?php echo Form::open('my/route'); ?>
```

The first parameter to the method is the URI we wish to submit the form to. The second parameter is the `METHOD` used to submit the form, if you don't provide a method as a string Laravel will assume that you want a `POST` form, which is the most common usage.

The third parameter is also optional. You can pass an array of `attribute => value` pairs to add extra attributes to the `<form>` tag. For example, if you wished to target the form with some Javascript you may want to pass `array('id' => 'myform')` as the third parameter to give the element an `id`.

To submit a form to a secure URI (https) you will need to use the `open_secure()` method instead of `open()`. It accepts the same parameters.

If you wish to be able to have files uploaded from your form then it will need to use `multipart/data` We can use `open_for_files()` instead of the `open()` method to accomplish this. This method also accepts the same parameters.

Finally if you wish to submit to a secure URI and have files uploaded you will need to use the `open_secure_for_files()` method. This once again accepts the same parameters and is a combination of both `open_secure()` and `open_for_files()`.

6.2 Adding Labels

The next line contains the `Form::label()` method which is used to create a `<label>` element. The first parameter is the `name` of the input element that it describes to be used in the `for=""` attribute. The second parameter is what will be used as the content of the `label` element. You can pass an array as an optional third parameter to apply extra HTML element attributes.

6.3 Generating Inputs

Next we have the input generators, these methods help to generate all of the HTML elements that are common to forms. In the example above we use the `text()` and `password()` method to generate `<input type="text"`.. and `<input type="password"`.. elements.

The first parameter to the method, is the value of the elements name attribute. The optional second parameter is the default value of the element. Once more we can pass an array of HTML attributes as an optional third parameter. Are you starting to see a pattern yet?

The textarea() and hidden() methods also accept the same parameters as the text() method.

Check-boxes can be created using the checkbox() method, with the first parameter being the name of the element and the second being the value. The third option is an optional boolean switch to set whether the element is initially checked or not. It will default to false. The fourth optional parameter again sets attributes. In fact, go ahead and assume that all future inputs accept an attributes array as their optional final parameter. Let's have a look at a check-box generator..

```
1  <?php echo Form::checkbox('admin', 'yes', true, array('id' => 'admin-checke\
2  r')); ?>
```

The radio() method creates radio buttons and shares the same parameters as the checkbox() method.

Next we have drop downs, the most awkward of all form elements. Fortunately, all we need to do is pass a name, an array of value => label options, and an optional parameter to state which option should be selected by default to the select() method. Our drop-down will then be generated for us, for example..

```
1  <?php
2
3  Form::select('roles', array(
4          0 => 'User',
5          1 => 'Member',
6          2 => 'Editor',
7          3 => 'Administrator'
8  ), 2);
```

and we get..

```
1  <select name="roles">
2          <option value="0">User</option>
3          <option value="1">Member</option>
4          <option value="2" selected="selected">Editor</option>
5          <option value="3">Administrator</option>
6  </select>
```

Great! Now it's time to submit our form.

6.4 Generating Buttons

The submit() and button() generator methods both accept the same parameters. The first being the value of the HTML element, and the second being the usual array of attributes.

```php
<?php

Form::submit('Login');
Form::button('Do other thing!');
```

6.5 Secret Inputs

There are also a number of extra generation methods for less common form inputs that aren't covered by the documentation. Many of these inputs were added with the HTML5 spec, and are in the process of being implemented by good web browsers (not IE). Here is a listing of the methods along with their parameters.

```php
<?php

// create a search field
Form::search($name, $value = null, $attributes = array());

// a textbox that only allows email addresses
Form::email($name, $value = null, $attributes = array());

// this text field will only allow phone numbers
Form::telephone($name, $value = null, $attributes = array());

// valid URL's only
Form::url($name, $value = null, $attributes = array());

// a number field with rocker switches
Form::number($name, $value = null, $attributes = array());

// a date picker
Form::date($name, $value = null, $attributes = array());

// used for file uploads
Form::file($name, $attributes = array());
```

6.6 CSRF Token

If you intend to use the in built cross-site-request-forgery (CSRF) filter to protect your AJAX submitted forms, you can add the CSRF token to your form by using the method token(). For example..

```
1   <?php
2
3   Form::token();
```

6.7 Form Macros

Laravel has provided many different input methods, but what if we need something a little more custom? Fortunately Laravel has provided the macro() method to allow us to create our own input generators.

By passing an input name and a closure to the macro() method we can define our own input generator, let's take a look.

```
1   <?php
2
3   Form::macro('shoe_size', function() {
4           return '<input type="shoe_size" />';
5   });
```

Now we can use the Form class to generate our shoe size field in the same way as any other input, for example..

```
1   <?php echo Form::shoe_size(); ?>
```

If you need to use parameters, simply add them as parameters to the closure. Enjoy creating your own unique input generators!

7 Handling Input

Now that we know how to create forms, we need to learn how to handle the input that has been sent by them. As always, Laravel has provided an ultra clean way of dealing with your input data. No need to interact with PHP arrays such as $_POST, $_GET and $_FILES. Let's be honest, those look ugly.

7.1 Request data

Let's use the Input class to handle this instead.

```php
1   <?php
2
3   $panda = Input::get('panda');
```

Now we have a Panda! Great.. we have too many already. Due to an unfortunate welsh border breach, Wales is now infested with red pandas. They are everywhere, I'm using one as a footrest right now. How did you think Emma managed to snap up that cover shot, they come from China!

Anyway, let's get back on track. One thing that you need to remember about the get() method on the Input class is that it doesn't refer to $_GET data. You will see that get() is simply a nice and expressive short method name for retrieving all kinds of data. The Input class also responds to get() with all kinds of request data, including $_POST.

If a piece of request data isn't set, the Input class will return a null value. If you pass a second parameter to the get() method and the index doesn't exist then the method will return the second parameter instead. This means that you can use it without worrying about any undefined errors popping up. Very useful!

```php
1   <?php
2
3   $panda = Input::get('panda', 'Muffin');
```

Now if our panda doesn't have a name it will be called 'Muffin', awwww..

If you would like to retrieve the entire request array, just skip the index. Easy as that.

```php
1   <?php
2
3   $morepandas = Input::get();
```

By default the get() array won't includes values from the $_FILES array. However if you use all() instead of get() it will contain files too.

```php
1  <?php
2
3  $pandas_and_files = Input::all();
```

If you would like to check if a piece of post data exists without actually returning it, simply use the elegant and highly expressive has() method which will return a boolean result.

```php
1  <?php
2
3  $do_we_have_a_panda = Input::has('panda');
```

7.2 Files

To access an element from the $_FILES array, make a call to the Input::file() method, for example..

```php
1  <?php
2
3  $file = Input::file('spoon');
```

If you would like to retrieve a file attribute then add a period and an attribute key to the first parameter, for example to retrieve the file size..

```php
1  $size = Input::file('spoon.size');
```

Once again, calling the method without a parameter will retrieve the full array of files.

** Note: You can use this syntax to access all multi dimensional arrays. Simply use a period to denote a nested array index. **

```php
1  $files = Input::file();
```

7.3 Flash Data

Flash data is a useful method of storing data in the session for use in the next request. It can be a useful way to repopulate forms.

To flash all of the current request data to the session, for it to be accessible in the next request, simply use the flash() method.

```php
1  <?php
2
3  Input::flash();
```

If you only want to flash a portion of the current request data, just pass 'only' as the first parameter to the method and an array of field names that you wish flashed as the second parameter.

```php
<?php

Input::flash('only', array('betty', 'simon'));
```

Now we will take Betty and Simon with us to the next request. Alternatively we could specify a list of fields that we don't want to take with us using the except option, for example..

```php
<?php

Input::flash('except', array('uncle_bob'));
```

There, now we can leave Uncle Bob behind, he's an arrogant soul, and dislikes our new national animal the red panda.

Now we can use the standard Redirect::to() method to move to a new request. From here we can use the expressive Input::old() method to retrieve a value that has been flashed from a previous request.

```php
<?php

$betty = Input::old('betty');
```

As you can see, Betty has survived the transition. You can think of flash data as those fuzzy transporter pads from Star Trek, moving Kirk and his buddies from one request to the next.

Once again you can skip the parameter to return a full array of flash data.

```php
<?php

$people = Input::old();
```

You can use the had() method to see if an index of flash data exists.

```php
<?php

Input::had('uncle_bob');
```

Of course not, we hate Uncle Bob.

Laravel wouldn't be the framework it is without its wonderful short-cuts and expressive methods. Let's have a look at a prime example of this in action.

```php
1    <?php
2
3    return Redirect::to('party')->with_input();
```

The `with_input()` method will flash all of our request data for us, it also accepts the same `only` and `except` methods as our `flash()` method.

```php
1    <?php
2
3    return Redirect::to('party')->with_input('only', array('betty', 'simon'));
4    return Redirect::to('party')->with_input('except', array('uncle_bob'));
```

Now that you have access to form data, your applications will become much more interactive!

8 Validation

Validation is an important part of many web applications. You can never trust your users, they have been plotting to destroy you for weeks by abusing your forms with evil javascripts.

We can't let them win, they must not destroy our beautiful applications. Let's validate all input provided by the user, that way they won't be able to harm us at all.

Naturally Laravel has a library, aptly named 'Validation' that will do all the hard work for us.

8.1 Set up validation

Let's start by creating an imaginary form, close your eyes and imagine a nice long form with many fields... uh oh... how can I get you to open your eyes again..?

Right, I will assume you got fed up of waiting, have opened your eyes and are back with me again, along with our imaginary form. Let's get the input data from that form.

```php
1   <?php
2
3   $input = Input::get();
```

Now normally you don't want to use the `get()` method, as its an easy way to populate your input array with extra data you don't need. In fact the open source collaboration site github was a victim to mass assignment. I have used `get()` to simplify the tutorial. In your applications please build the input array only with the fields you need.

Our input array now contains something that looks a little like this..

```php
1   <?php
2
3   array(
4           'name' => 'John',
5           'age'  => 15
6   )
```

Let's validate these fields to make sure they make sense to our application. Before we can start the validation process we need to create a set of rules that will be used to validate each field. With the validator class, rules are defined in an array format. Let's jump right in and take a look.

```php
1   <?php
2
3   $rules = array(
4           'name'          => 'required|min:3|max:32|alpha',
5           'age'           => 'required|integer|min:16'
6   );
```

Great, now we have some rules. The array key is the field that is being validated upon, and the array value contains a number of validation rules separate by a pipe | symbol.

In our case we are validating that both fields contain a value by using the 'required' rule. The length of the user's name must be a minimum of 3 characters (min:3) and a maximum length of 32 characters (max:32). The 'alpha' rule will check to make sure that the name field only contains letters.

Our age field must contain an `integer` and the value must be at least `16`. You see that the `min` rule has adapted to fit the content that its validating, very clever!

Don't worry, we will cover all the validation rules later. For now let's see the validation in action, here we go.

```php
1   <?php
2
3   $v = Validator::make($input, $rules);
```

We have created our validator object with the `make()` method, passing it our input array and our rules array. Let's see if it validates!

```php
1    <?php
2
3    if( $v->fails() )
4    {
5           // code for validation failure :(
6    }
7    else
8    {
9           // code for validation success!
10   }
```

As you can see, we use the `fails()` method to check the result of the validation attempt, it will return `true` if the validation has failed and `false` if it was successful.

If you prefer a more positive outlook on your validations, you could use the `passes()` method, which returns the opposite values..

```php
1    <?php
2
3    if( $v->passes() )
4    {
5           // code for validation success!
6    }
7    else
8    {
9           // code for validation failure :(
10   }
```

There, now we are positive and can dance over rainbows with sparkleponies.

8.2 Errors

If your validation fails, which it will because our user is under 16 (sorry for slaying your sparklepony), you will want to find out what went wrong. The validator provides an `errors` Messages object which allows us to easily find the information we need.

The `errors` object has similar methods to the `Input` class, so I will not need to go over them all. Let's retrieve an array of errors for a specific field.

```php
1   <?php
2
3   $age_errors = $v->errors->get('age');
```

Now we have an array containing all of the errors associated with the age field..

```php
1   <?php
2
3   array(
4           'The age must be at least 16.'
5   )
```

Most of the time I find myself using the `first()` method in my views, which returns the first array item if it exists, or null if it doesn't. For example..

```php
1   <?php echo Form::label('username', 'Username') ?>
2   <?php echo $errors->first('username') ?>
3   <?php echo Form::text('username') ?>
```

Now our validation errors will appear for this field if any are present. You can also pass a second parameter to the `first()` method to format the output..

```php
1   <?php echo $errors->first('username', '<span class="error">:message</span>'\
2   ) ?>
```

Neat!

You can also use `has()` to check to see if an error exists, and `all()` to retrieve all errors as an array.

8.3 Validation Rules

Here is a list of validation rules, and their purpose.

required

Ensure that a value for a field is present, and is not an empty string.

alpha

The string must only consist of letters (alphabetical characters).

alpha_num

The string must only contain letters and numbers. Useful for usernames.

alpha_dash

The string must contain only letters, numbers, dashes or underscore characters. Useful for storing URL slugs.

size:5

(string) The string must be exactly five characters long. (numeric) The value must be five.

between:5,10

(string) The length of the string must be between five and ten characters. (numeric) The value must be between five and ten.

min:5

(string) The length of the string must be between five characters or more. (numeric) The value must be equal to or greater than five. (file) The file size must be 5 kilobytes or more.

max:5

(string) The length of the string must be less than or equal to five. (numeric) The value must be less than or equal to five. (file) The file size must be 5 kilobytes or less.

numeric

The value must be numeric.

integer

The value must be an integer or whole number.

in:red,green,blue

Ensure that the value is contained within the list of values provided.

not_in:pink,purple

Ensure that none of the values provided match the value.

confirmed

The value of the field must match a confirmation field, named in the format '

accepted

The field value must be equal to 'yes' or 1. Useful for validating check-boxes.

same:age

The field value must match the field specified by the same rule.

different:age

The field value must not match the field specified by the same rule.

match:/[a-z]+/

The field value must match the provided regular expression.

unique:users

This is one of my favourites. The validator will look at the `users` database table, and make sure that the value is unique within the column that has the same name as the field name. Useful for making sure that duplicate usernames or email addresses don't occur.

If you would like to specify an alternate column name, simply pass it as a second parameter..

```
1   unique:users,nickname
```

You can also force the rule to ignore a provided `id` by passing it as a third parameter.

```
1   unique:users,nickname,5
```

exists:colors

Acts as the opposite of `unique`, the value must already exist in the database table. Once more you can pass a second parameter to refer to another column.

before:1984-12-12

The date provided by the field, must have occurred before the date template provided to the `before` rule.

The before and after filters use strtotime() to calculate a timestamp for comparison, this means you can do some neat tricks like..

```
1   before:next Thursday
```

Unfortunately I was on the one that added this functionality, so if it breaks you can go ahead and shout at me... sorry!

after:1984-12-12

Similar to before, only the date must occur after the date provided to the `after` rule.

email

The value must be a valid email address.

url

The value must match the format of an URL.

active_url

The value must match a valid active URL. `checkdnsr` is used to verify that the URL is active.

mimes:png,mp3

The value must be a `$_FILE` which whose MIME type matches the file extensions provided. You can add additional MIME types to the array in `config/mimes.php`.

image

The uploaded file must be an image.

8.4 Custom Error Messages

I find the default error messages quite descriptive, but your clients might have their own ideas. Let's see how we can customize our error messages to suit our needs.

You can edit the validation error messages directly by modifying the file `application/language/en/validation.php`...

```
1   ...
2   "after"        => "The :attribute must be a date after :date.",
3   "alpha"        => "The :attribute may only contain letters.",
4   "alpha_dash"   => "The :attribute may only contain letters, numbers, and \
5   dashes.",
6   ...
```

Laravel replaces the `:attribute` marker with the name of the field. Other markers also exist within the rules, and their purpose is quite self explanatory.

If you would rather change the messages for a single form, rather than edit them globally, you can pass a third array of messages to the `Validator::make()` method.

```
1   <?php
2
3   $messages = array(
4       'same'   => 'The :attribute and :other must match, fool!',
5       'size'   => 'The :attribute must be exactly :size , like duh!'
6   );
7
8   $v = Validator::make($input, $rules, $messages);
```

Great now we have custom messages! We can even specify error messages for individual fields by setting the message key to `field_rule`, for example..

```php
1   <?php
2
3   $messages = array(
4       'age_required'    => 'You need to have had at least one birthday!'
5   );
```

8.5 Custom Validation Rules

The validator allows you add extra rules to suit the needs of your application, let's jump right in and take a look at how we register a new validation rule.

```php
1   <?php
2
3   Validator::register('superdooper', function($attribute, $value, $parameters\
4   ){
5           return $value == 'superdooper';
6   });
```

Our newly created validation rule superdooper will ensure that our value matches the string 'superdooper'. Your custom validations should return true on success, or false on failure.

The $attribute value will be the name of the field being validated, and $value will of course contain the value.

The $parameters attribute contains an array of parameters that have been passed to the rule after the colon, and separated by commas.

As you have created a new validator, there will be no error messages associated with it yet, we will need to add one so that Laravel knows what to say when it fails. We can add an error message in the same way as we have previously..

```php
1   <?php
2
3   'superdooper' => 'The :attribute must be superdooper, ok trooper?!',
```

Once again you can pass the extra error message array as a third parameter to the Validator::make() method, or simply add it to your application/language/en/validation.php file for safe keeping.

8.6 Validation Classes

If we want to provide many new validation methods, or reuse them across a number if projects, it would be best to create a validation class. Validation classes extend Laravel's data, and overload it with additional validation methods. The class is created in the application/libraries directory for easy loading, but you could place it elsewhere as long as it is registered with the Autoloader (later chapter). Let's take a look at the class.

```php
1    <?php
2
3    // application/libraries/validator.php
4
5    class Validator extends Laravel\Validator {
6
7        public function validate_awesome($attribute, $value, $parameters)
8        {
9            return $value == 'awesome';
10        }
11
12   }
```

As you can see our Validator class extends the Laravel\Validator name-spaced core class and provides additional validations in the form of validate_<rulename> methods. The validation methods accept the same parameters as the Validator::register() closure, and work in the same way.

In order to use our new validation class, we will need to remove the existing alias for Validator from our application/config/application.php file. This way Laravel will use our created class instead of the one in the Laravel source folder.

You could use this method to replace the original validation methods with your own, for example you could create a validate_size method and calculate the size in an alternate format.

I would suggest adding custom error messages to the validation language file when using Validation classes, this will allow for a much easier migration to another project, and will not require any 'source-digging' to find all the messages used.

9 Migrations

Originally I had attempted to include a guide to the Fluent Query Builder with this chapter, but I now feel that the chapter has become too long, so I have decided to cover database set-up and migrations only in this chapter. Get ready for a nice long explanation of Fluent in the next chapter.

Migrations are one of my favourite Laravel features. I hate writing SQL, and the Schema class allows me to create my tables easily without writing a single line of that foul "language"! Not only that, but the Schema code also looks absolutely beautiful and reads like a book.

If you have not encountered migrations before, they are a way of describing changes to your database in files so that different installations / development copies of your application are aware of the current schema. Changes to the schema can also be reverted or 'rolled back'. Migrations can also be used to populate tables with example data (also known as seeding).

9.1 Database Setup

Head over to your `application/config/database.php` configuration file. If you have ever installed a PHP application you will be familiar with this kind of file. You have your database access credentials to hand don't you? If not go dig them out right now!

Are you back yet? Great, let's take a closer look.

Scroll down to the 'connections' array key, here you will see a number of options for a few different type of databases. Fill in the connection parameters for your database of choice, I am going to stick to good ol' fashioned mySQL.

```php
1   <?php
2
3   'mysql' => array(
4           'driver'   => 'mysql',
5           'host'     => 'localhost',
6           'database' => 'codefun',
7           'username' => 'root',
8           'password' => 'pandaseatbamboo',
9           'charset'  => 'utf8',
10          'prefix'   => '',
11  ),
```

There we go, now you will want to scroll up a little bit, and change the 'default' array key to reflect the database you are using. For me it's already on mySQL.

```php
1   <?php
2
3   'default' => 'mysql',
```

Now we have our database configured, we need some tables to play with. Onwards to migrations!

9.2 Migrations

Let's get started by creating a migration file.

We are going to use Laravel's command line interface artisan to create our new migration. To run Artisan you will need to have PHP CLI installed. Normally this will be installed along side your web server. You will also need to open a terminal to the root of your Laravel package where the 'artisan' file exists. Right, let's type our first artisan command :

```
1  php artisan migrate:make create_users
```

We are telling artisan to run the make method on the migrate task. We pass a name for our migration to identify it by, I like to name it after the action being performed. In this case we are creating the users table.

Let's have a look at the result.

```
1  Great! New migration created!
```

Enthusiastic! If we take a look in our application/migrations directory, we will see a new file named 2012_03_30_220459_create_users.php. Well yours might not be called that! You see artisan takes the current date, and adds the time in His format to create the file name. The reason for this is that dates are very important to migrations (and single people). The system needs to be able to know in which order to apply the changes.

Let's open up the file and take a look at the migration class.

```
1  <?php
2
3  class Create_Users {
4
5      /**
6       * Make changes to the database.
7       *
8       * @return void
9       */
10     public function up()
11     {
12             //
13     }
14
15     /**
16      * Revert the changes to the database.
17      *
18      * @return void
19      */
```

```
20      public function down()
21      {
22              //
23      }
24
25  }
```

As you can see, our migration class consists of two methods. up() is responsible for making all of your database changes, where down() accomplishes the exact reverse. This way a migration can be performed, and rolled back when necessary. If you were to create a table within the up() method, we would DROP the same table in the down() method.

So how do we perform changes on our database, no doubt with some complex ugly SQL query right? Haha, no. We are using Laravel, if it's ugly, it's not in the framework. Let's have a look at creating a table with the Laravel Schema class.

```php
1   <?php
2
3   Schema::create('users', function($table) {
4           // auto incremental id (PK)
5           $table->increments('id');
6
7           // varchar 32
8           $table->string('username', 32);
9           $table->string('email', 255);
10          $table->string('password', 64);
11
12          // int
13          $table->integer('role');
14
15          // boolean
16          $table->boolean('active');
17
18          // created_at | updated_at DATETIME
19          $table->timestamps();
20  });
```

We call the create() method on the Schema class to create a new table, and pass the name of the table to be created, and a closure as parameters. We also need to pass a parameter to the closure. You can call it whatever you like, but I like using $table because I think it makes the code read better.

Inside the closure, we can use the $table parameter to create our fields with a number of handy, well-named methods. Let's take a quick look at them.

increments()

Add an auto-incrementing ID to the table, most of your tables will have this!

string()

Create a VARCHAR field, string sounds a lot better doesn't it?

integer()

Add an integer field to the table.

float()

Add a float field to the table.

boolean()

Add a boolean field to the table.

date()

Add a date field to the table.

timestamp()

Add a timestamp field to the table.

timestamps()

Add created_at and updated_at timestamp fields.

text()

Add a text field to the table.

blob()

Add a blob data field to the table.

You can also use the chainable method ->nullable() to allow the field to receive NULL values.

Full details on the parameters available to the above methods can be found in the official documentation[1].

Great, so now we have created our table! Since we created the table in the up() method, we now need to DROP the table in the down() method, so that the schema will return to its original form after a roll-back. Fortunately the Schema class has another method that is perfect for this task.

```php
1  <?php
2
3  Schema::drop('users');
```

Yep, it doesn't get easier than that. The Schema class also has functions for performing other schema tasks, such as dropping columns drop_column(), adding indexes unique() and a number of foreign key methods. I think that covering all of them here would turn the book into an API, something I don't wish to do, besides they are explained well in the official documentation[2], and if you take a look there we can move on to new things. How about finding out how we run these migrations? Let's do it!

---

[1] http://laravel.com/docs/database/migrations

[2] http://laravel.com/docs/database/schema

Before we can run our migrations, we need to install the `laravel_migrations` table so that Laravel can keep track of which migrations have been run. Fortunately artisan has a command which will perform the necessary database changes for you. Let's have a go.

```
1   php artisan migrate:install
```

And the result..

```
1   Migration table created successfully.
```

Great! Now that the `laravel_migrations` table has been created we can finally run our new migration. Simply use the task name this time, here we go.

```
1   php artisan migrate
2   Migrated: application/2012_03_30_220459_create_users
```

Whoop! If we take a look at our database we will see that the users table has been created successfully. Wait, we made a mistake! (we didn't, but I like drama and I need an excuse to use roll-back) Let's roll-back our schema to redo the changes.

```
1   php artisan migrate:rollback
2   Rolled back: application/2012_03_30_220459_create_users
```

Please note that if you would like to provide example data to populate your database with, simply create it with the Fluent Query Builder which will be covered in a later chapter.

Easy as pie! Now that you know how to use migrations, you can build your schema and populate your database whenever you please! In the next chapter we will be looking at the Fluent Query Builder.

10 Fluent Query Builder

Fluent is another wonderful library that Laravel provides to help me dodge the SQL bullet, although you can still write raw SQL statements if you happen to enjoy pain. The best part about using Fluent, apart from the lack of SQL, is that it uses prepared statements which are fully protected against SQL injection. Fluent is also... well fluent in a number of different SQL dialects, so your methods will work across a variety of databases. Before we get started you will need to understand the concept of method chaining, take a look at this example.

```php
1  <?php
2
3  Class::make()->chain()->chain()->chain()->trigger();
```

This is a very useful way of stringing options together, and is a lovely way of expressing SQL (as you will see later). The class is instantiated with the make() method. Sometimes you will also pass 'startup parameters' to the class this way. The chain() methods are used to modify the request with different options, and the trigger() method is used to bring back the final result. This might sound a bit confusing, but let's take a look at an example from fluent.

```php
1  <?php
2
3  $users = DB::table('users')->where('username', '=', 'dayle')->get();
```

The above example will execute a simple..

```
1  SELECT * FROM users WHERE username = 'dayle';
```

and bring back an array of objects, representing database rows that are the result of the query.

The table() method is instantiating the object, and setting the table that we intend to work with. The where() is a chain method that applies a WHERE clause to our query, and get() is the final trigger method that retrieves all objects that are the result of the query.

The get() trigger will bring back an array of results, so lets start by looping the result set with a foreach.

```php
1  <?php
2
3  foreach ($users as $user)
4  {
5          echo $user->email;
6  }
```

As you can see in the above example, fields for the row are accessed using the attributes of the result object. The loop above would output the email addresses for all of our users.

10.1 Retrieving Results

Let's have a look at some of the other trigger methods for retrieving results.

get()

We have just used this, it will bring back all objects which are the result of the query in an array.

first()

This trigger will bring back a single result object. The first object to match the requirements of the query.

find($id)

This trigger will find the item by its database id. This is a handy shortcut to where('id', '=', $id). It will bring back a single result object.

only($fieldname)

This will bring back the result for a single field matching the query.

get(array())

Pass an array of fields to get() to retrieve only those fields.

10.2 Where Clauses

So now we have the methods that we need to retrieve our database results, how can we apply conditions to these SQL queries? Well in the example above you saw me using the where() method, let's take a closer look at this.

```php
1  <?php
2
3  $users = DB::table('users')->where('username', '=', 'dayle')->get();
```

Here we have the same snippet again, but we are concentrating on the where() part of the chain :

```php
1  <?php
2
3  where('username', '=', 'dayle')
```

The great thing about how Laravel handles the where clause is that the chain looks a little bit like the SQL being generated. In the chain method above we are saying WHERE username = 'dayle'. The first parameter to the method states the field which we are comparing, the second parameter states the operator to use for the comparison, and the third parameter is the value which we are comparing with. We could also use :

```php
1   <?php
2
3   where('age', '>', '18')
4   // WHERE age > '18'
5   // Drink up! Not if you are American though, sorry.
```

What if we want more conditions? Well first we need to decide if we need 'AND WHERE' or 'OR WHERE'. To include an 'AND' where clause, simply use the where() method again in the chain, for example :

```php
1   <?php
2
3   $users = DB::table('users')
4                       ->where('username', '=', 'dayle')
5                       ->where('sexyness', '>', 5000)
6                       ->get();
```

As you can see in the above example, I have put each chain method on a new line. I find this is easier to read, and avoids having terribly long lines of code. This chain will perform the following SQL :

```sql
1   SELECT * FROM users WHERE username = 'dayle' AND sexyness > 5000;
```

If we would prefer to use an OR where condition we simply use the or_where() method, which accepts the same parameters. For example :

```php
1   <?php
2
3   $users = DB::table('users')
4                       ->where('username', '=', 'dayle')
5                       ->or_where('face', 'LIKE', '%malemodel%')
6                       ->get();
```

which gives us :

```sql
1   SELECT * FROM users WHERE username = 'dayle' OR face LIKE '%malemodel%';
```

Now I don't need to explain how every feature of SQL works, there are plenty of other books for that. I will however name the methods used to accomplish common tasks instead.

Use the where_in(), where_not_in(), or_where_in() and or_where_not_in() methods to match a field to one of an array of items.

The where_null(), where_not_null(), or_where_null(), and or_where_not_null() methods to match a field to a NULL value.

Sometimes you will want to nest where clauses together, Laravel provides functionality for this in the form of 'Nested Where Clauses'. Let's take a look at a code example..

```php
1   <?php
2
3   $users = DB::table('users')
4          ->where('id', '=', 1)
5          ->or_where(function($query)
6          {
7                  $query->where('age', '>', 25);
8                  $query->where('votes' '>', 100);
9          })
10         ->get();
```

By passing a closure containing extra where clauses to another where method, we can create nested where clauses. The result can be seen in the SQL:

```sql
1   SELECT * FROM "users" WHERE "id" = ? OR ("age" > ? AND "votes" > ?)
```

neat huh?

And now for a more interesting feature! (I told you about how I loathe SQL right?) Dynamic where clauses give you a really funky way of defining simple where clauses. Check this out..

```php
1   <?php
2
3   where_size(5)->get();
```

Here we are specifying the field to compare in the method name. Fluent is so clever that it will deal with it, no problem!

It will even understand AND and OR, check this out!

```php
1   <?php
2
3   where_size_and_height(700, 400)->get();
```

Expressive, clean, Laravel at its finest.

10.3 Table Joins

Let's have a look at a join using Fluent.

```php
1   <?php
2
3   DB::table('tasks')
4          ->join('project', 'tasks.id', '=', 'project.task_id')
5          ->get(array('task.name', 'project.name'));
```

We pass the name of the join table as the first parameter, and use the remaining three parameters to perform an 'ON' clause, similar to how we perform 'WHERE's.

We then pass the fields we want to return to the get() method as an array.

We can do a left_join() exactly the same way, in fact it takes the same parameters, easy huh?

Do you remember the nested where clauses? Well you can use a similar technique to add more conditions to the ON clause of a join. Let's take a look.

```php
<?php

DB::table('tasks')
        ->join('project', function($join) {
                $join->on('tasks.id', '=', 'project.task_id');
                $join->or_on('tasks.author_id', '=', 'project.author_id');
        })
        ->get(array('task.name', 'project.name'));
```

In this case, we pass a closure as the second parameter to the join() method, then use the on(), or_on() and and_on() methods to set the conditions.

10.4 Ordering

Ordering is pretty important, you don't wanna waste resources doing that with PHP. You could... sure... lots of nasty array_sort()ing, tons of loops, that wouldn't be any fun. Let's pass this responsibility to fluent.

```php
<?php

DB::table('shoes')->order_by('size', 'asc')->get();
```

Hmm shoes? Women are meant to think about shoes but thats all that came to mind.. scarey. Anyway its as easy as passing a field name and either asc for ascending, or desc for descending. To sort on more columns simply repeat the order_by() chain.

10.5 Limiting.. no Taking

What if we only want to get a certain number of results back? In SQL we would use LIMIT bah that sounds stupid, Laravel provides take().

```php
<?php

DB::table('shoes')->take(10)->get();
```

Now I want 10 shoes? I should be more worried.. But it's clear, limiting is very simple!

10.6 Skipping Results

We don't need the first 5 pairs of shoes do we? They are leather shoes and I like to wear skate shoes. Very wide feet you see.. Let's just skip them.

```php
<?php

DB::table('shoes')->skip(5)->get();
```

There we go, now we can skip() the first 5 results. Easy as pie!

10.7 Aggregates

Sometimes its handy to run basic maths on queries. AVG, MIN, MAX, SUM, and COUNT are used all the time to quickly get the result we want with SQL, and they are all available with the Fluent Query Builder. Let's take a look.

```php
<?php

$val = DB::table('shoes')->avg('size');
$val = DB::table('shoes')->min('size');
$val = DB::table('shoes')->max('size');
$val = DB::table('shoes')->sum('size');
$val = DB::table('shoes')->count();
```

Simple! Don't forget that these are trigger methods. We don't need to add get() here. You are also welcome to add conditions with where() or whatever you like!

10.8 Expressions

The methods we have been using so far escape and quote the parameters you provide automatically, but what if we need something really custom? What if we don't want anything else added? For this we can use the DB::raw() method. Here's an example :

```php
<?php

DB::table('shoes')->update(array('worn' => DB::raw('NOW()')));
```

In this query the NOW() will not be escaped or quoted. Lots of freedom there, but don't forget that spiderman quote! Be responsible with this power.

10.9 ++ (or decrementing)

What if we want to simply increment or decrement a value? Easy as pie!

```php
1   <?php
2
3   DB::table('shoes')->increment('size');
4   DB::table('shoes')->decrement('size');
```

Simply pass a field name, and voila!

10.10 Insert

Finally, let's store some data. All this time we have been looking at reading data but this will be more fun! Well it's quite simple really. To insert a new row all we have to do is provide a key-value array to the insert() method, which is a trigger method by the way!

```php
1   <?php
2
3   DB::table('shoes')->insert(array(
4           'color'         => 'hot pink',
5           'type'          => 'heels',
6           'size'          => '12'
7   ));
```

Wait, lets grab the id thats created with this new row, it might be handy later? We can use insert_get_id() with the same parameters for this.

```php
1   <?php
2
3   $id = DB::table('shoes')->insert_get_id(array(
4           'color'         => 'hot pink',
5           'type'          => 'heels',
6           'size'          => '12'
7   ));
```

That's my weekend pair, let's keep this between us. We now have a nice hot pink pair of heels in size 12, stored in the shoes table of our database.

10.11 Update

Wait, did I say heels in that last section? They were hot pink skate shoes! If only we could go back and fix our mistake. I could update the table and no one would see my shame. Oh I guess we could probably use the `update()` method, you see it takes an array with the same syntax as `insert()`.

```php
1  <?php
2
3  DB::table('shoes')->update(array(
4       'type'         => 'skate shoes'
5  ));
```

Hold on, we aren't specifying a record here. I don't want to change all my records to skate shoes, it would ruin my wonderful Laravel flip flops. Let's use a `where()` method and that `$id` we got earlier to narrow it down to the record we want. Chain time!

```php
1  <?php
2
3  DB::table('shoes')
4       ->where('id', '=', $id)
5       ->update(array(
6            'type'         => 'skate shoes'
7       ));
```

There, we fixed the problem before anyone noticed.

10.12 Delete

To delete a row (please, not the shoes, they are innocent!) we can use the `delete()` method with a `where()` clause, or simply pass it an `id` directly to delete a single row. Let's see these methods in action.

```php
1  <?php
2
3  DB::table('not_shoes')->where('texture', '=', 'fuzzy')->delete();
```

Simple. The fuzzy things are now gone!

```php
1  <?php
2
3  DB::table('shoes')->delete($id);
```

NO! Not the hot pink skate shoes. You have obviously learned too much, please keep the responsibility and power thing in mind. We don't want any more shoe massacres.

In the next chapter, we will be moving on from sho... Fluent, and taking a look at Eloquent. Eloquent will allow us to treat our database rows as objects, and provides an elegant.. or eloquent solution to handling relationships.

11 Eloquent ORM

An ORM is a really useful package, it stands for Object Relational Mapper. Sounds pretty complicated right? Let's break it down a little. (add bass beat) The mapper part, is because we are mapping our PHP objects or classes to database tables and rows. The Relational part will become clear in the relationships section.

There are many ORM solutions out there, but none as Eloquent as... well Eloquent. Eloquent ships with Laravel, and can be used out of the box. For this portion I am going to assume that you set up your database as described in the `Migrations` chapter, and that you are familiar with the methods and chaining from the `Fluent Query Builder` chapter. We are going to build on these.

You see Eloquent is an alternative to using Fluent, but it shares many of the same methods. The only difference is that we are going to be interacting with Eloquent models as results, rather than the `stdObject` we get back from Fluent. It's going to make our code look even clearer. Let's dive right in and check out the Eloquent model.

11.1 Creating and using Eloquent Models

```php
<?php

// application/models/user.php

class User extends Eloquent
{

}
```

Actually thats it.. no really, I am serious. You see, Eloquent trusts you. It knows that you have already created a nice migration for the users table. It doesn't need you to tell it about the fields that exist. It's going to trust that you know them. You should, you wrote the migration and made the table. Oh by the way, you did put an `increments('id')` in your table right? This is a common practice and Eloquent needs this to work.

Another thing you might have noticed about the model is that the class is called `User` and the table is called `users`. This isn't a typo. Eloquent is so clever that it can detect the plurals for the English language. Our object is singular, so we define it as a `User`. However our database table `users` will contain any number of users, so Laravel knows to look for a table with a plural of the object name.

You may have picked up on the fact that it only detects plurals for the English language. What if you use another language, or a certain plural doesn't work for you? Simply add the word and its plural version to the array in the `application/config/strings.php` file. Now it will work as expected!

Maybe you don't like having the table name as plural form? Not a problem, simply use the static `$table` class attribute to specify another table name. For example..

```php
1    <?php
2
3    class User extends Eloquent
4    {
5            public static $table = 'app_users';
6    }
```

Right, typing that huge model definition must have worn you out (please note the sarcasm). Let's have a go at using our new model.

```php
1    <?php
2
3    $user = User::find(1);
```

Wait hold on... we have seen this before. Do you remember find() from our Fluent chapter? It brings back a single result by its primary key. You will find that Eloquent uses many of the methods used by Fluent. This is really convenient because you can use a combination of both database libraries without forgetting which method is for what. Sweet!

For eloquent simply use the object's name, and supply a static method. We don't need to use DB::table() for this one.

You can use the result object in a similar way. The truth is you are now interacting with an Eloquent object, but you couldn't really tell the difference at this point. Let's get that users name.

```php
1    <?php
2
3    echo $user->name;
```

Yep thats the same as last time. Nice and easy.

What if we would rather have our User object returned as an array? Simply call the to_array() method on any Eloquent model to receive an array instead of an object.

```php
1    <?php
2
3    $user = $user->to_array();
```

If you want to exclude certain fields from this array, you could add a $hidden static attribute to your Eloquent model, containing an array of all the fields to exclude. For example :

```php
1    <?php
2
3    class User extends Eloquent
4    {
5            public static $hidden = array('nickname');
6    }
```

Say we want multiple results back? We can use the fancy `all()` method to bring back every user, then we can have a sexy user party.

```php
1  <?php
2
3  $users = User::all();
```

What we now have is an array of user objects. We can loop through them to access each one individually. Simple as that.

```php
1  <?php
2
3  foreach ($users as $user)
4  {
5          add_to_sexy_party($user);
6  }
```

Nice, its really swinging in here. Quite a few guys though.. Well let's increase our chances and get rid of the other guys. Then it really will be a sexy party!

```php
1  <?php
2
3  $sexy_users = User::where('sex', '=', 'female')->get();
```

Whoop, lots better! The eye-candy threshold went up significantly. You see we just used a `where()` chain method and `get()` just like we did with fluent. There is nothing new there, just increased clarity.

I could cover all the query methods again for returning results, but I don't really need to. Simply flick back a chapter and mentally replace the word Fluent with Eloquent. You will get the idea.

Instead, let's see what has changed. Creating and updating objects (rows) just got a whole lot easier!

```php
1  <?php
2
3  $user = new User();
4
5  $user->name = 'Captain Sexypants';
6  $user->mojo = '100%';
7
8  $user->save();
```

Best not to invite Captain Sexypants to our party, we won't get any action with him around. Even his parrot has swagger.

You see we simply create a new User object, set class attributes for the fields that exist (we don't need to set the ID, Eloquent handles that) and save() the object to write our changes to the database. This is commonly known as the Active Record design pattern. It's a really nice way of interacting with our rows by treating them the same as any other object in our application. It's like the database and all that nasty SQL doesn't even exist!

If we already have a key-value array describing our friend 'Captain Sexypants' then we can either pass it as a constructor parameter to the new object, or use the mass-assignment method fill() to add him to the database. Check this out..

```php
1    <?php
2
3    $user = new User(array(
4            'name' => 'Captain Sexypants',
5            'mojo' => '100%'
6    ));
7
8    $user->save();
```

or

```php
1    <?php
2
3    $arr = array(
4            'name' => 'Captain Sexypants',
5            'mojo' => '100%'
6    );
7
8    $user = new User();
9    $user->fill($arr);
10   $user->save();
```

Please be careful not to let any extra information slip through when using mass-assignment as it could result in a potential security risk.

So what about updating a row? It's very similar, except we need to query for the user we want to change first. Let's see..

```php
1    <?php
2
3    $user = User::where('name', '=', 'Captain Sexypants')->first();
```

Here we use first() because we want to make sure we only get one object back. We can't change the values on an array, we would have to loop through each one and that would make a longer example than we need!

```php
1   <?php
2
3   $user->mojo = '5%';
4   $user->save();
```

Well I couldn't take all his mojo, that wouldn't be fair. At least he can come to the party now. So you see, updating is performed exactly the same way as inserting except that we need to find the object that we want to update first.

Do you remember using $table->timestamps() with in the migrations chapter to make updated_at and created_at fields? Eloquent will update these automatically for you, inserting a timestamp when an object is created and updating the updated_at field every time you save. If you would like to disable this feature simply add the $timestamps class attribute to your model and set it to false.

```php
1   <?php
2
3   class User extends Eloquent
4   {
5           public static $timestamps = false;
6   }
```

11.2 Relationships

Relationships are beautiful. No I haven't gone all soppy. I mean relationships between tables. In Eloquent they are beautiful. None of that 'JOIN' rubbish! We can define 'one-to-one', 'one-to-many' and 'many-to-many' just by adding some simple methods to our Eloquent Models. Let's jump right in. You will learn more with a code snippet in front of you.

On To One

Jumping right in..

```php
1   <?php
2
3   class User extends Eloquent
4   {
5           public function invite()
6           {
7                   return $this->has_one('Invite');
8           }
9   }
```

Let's go ahead and assume that we have made an `invites` table and an `Invite` model to contain our sexy party invites.

We have created a new public method called `invite()`, which will return `$this->has_-one('Invite')` to find a users invite via a has one relationship.

Now we can retrieve a user's (or party guest) invite with a clear expressive syntax. Let's take a peek:

```php
1   <?php
2
3   $invite = User::find(1)->invite()->first();
```

Again we are using `first()` because we only want one result. You see by adding `->invite()->` to the chain, which is of course our relationship method name, we retrieve the `Invite` object that is related to our `user`.

This relationship will execute two queries :

```sql
1   SELECT * FROM "users" WHERE "id" = 1;
2   SELECT * FROM "invites" WHERE "user_id" = 1;
```

From the query you will see that Eloquent is looking for `user_id` automatically as the foreign key. So if we want to use this relationship, we will need to create a `user_id` integer field with our migration, in the `Invites` table. What if we want to call our foreign key something else? No problem! We simply pass a second parameter to the `has_one()` method (or other relationship methods) to specify the new field name. For example..

```php
1   <?php
2
3   class User extends Eloquent
4   {
5           public function invite()
6           {
7                   return $this->has_one('Invite', 'the_invite_id');
8           }
9   }
```

What about the inverse of this relationship? What if we have an Invite, but we want to know who it `belongs` to? This is where the `belongs_to()` method comes in handy. Let's take a look at the model.

```php
1   <?php
2
3   class Invite extends Eloquent
4   {
```

```
5          public function user()
6          {
7                  return $this->belongs_to('User');
8          }
9   }
```

A similar syntax, but using `belongs_to()` instead to point out that the foreign key exists in this table.

Now we can use..

```
1   <?php
2
3   $user = Invite::find(1)->user()->first();
```

Easy!

One To Many

What if we want to return many related items? Well as you may have guessed from the header there's a method for that. Let's take a look. (I say that a lot don't I? Maybe it can be my catchphrase.)

```
1   <?php
2
3   Class User extends Eloquent
4   {
5          public function hats()
6          {
7                  return $this->has_many('Hat');
8          }
9   }
```

Again, you will see that we are passing the object name in string format with capitalisation to the `has_many()` method.

In this example the `hats` table will need a `user_id` foreign key. We can then use..

```
1   <?php
2
3   $hats = User::find(1)->hats()->get();
```

Note that we could also use a dynamic property with the same name to retrieve the same results with a shorter syntax. For example :

```
1   <?php
2
3   $hats = User::find(1)->hats;
```

Nicer still!

As before, you can pass another foreign key as a second parameter to use that instead. Let's move on!

Many To Many

Here things will get a little more complicated, but don't worry.. I am here to get you through this. Take my hand Wendy. Let's imagine that we have two Eloquent models, User and Task. A user may have many tasks, and a task may have many users. For this type of relationship we will need a third table.

This table is known by many names. A pivot table, a lookup table, an intermediate table, or el pivote grande.

It's simply a table with two integer fields user_id and task_id, that links the two tables together. This forms a many to many relationship.

The table is named after both related tables in a plural form, in an alphabetical order. Sounds complicated but it looks simple, check it out:

tasks_users

Great, now that we have our table, let's form the relationship:

```
1   <?php
2
3   class User extends Eloquent
4   {
5           public function tasks()
6           {
7                   return $this->has_many_and_belongs_to('Task');
8           }
9   }
```

again, similar syntax, with a slightly longer method name.

This time we can pass an optional second parameter to specify a different pivot table name. Simple.

11.3 Inserting Related Models

When we are inserting related models, we can set the user_id or hat_id foreign key ourselves, but thats not very pretty. Why not pass the object instead?

```php
1   <?php
2
3   $hat = Hat::find(1);
4   $user = User::find(1);
5   $user->hats()->insert($hat);
```

That looks a lot better! It's like handing objects to each other and is much cleaner than dealing with those integer foreign keys directly.

With has_many() relationships you can pass an array of field-value pairs to the save() method to insert or update related models. For example:

```php
1   <?php
2
3   $hat = array(
4           'name'                  => 'Dennis',
5           'style'         => 'Fedora'
6   );
7
8   $user = User::find(1);
9
10  $user->hats()->save($hat);
```

Clean!

When we are creating a new related item with a many-to-many relationship, if we use the insert() method Eloquent will not only create the new object, but also update the pivot table with the new entry. For example :

```php
1   <?php
2
3   $hat = array(
4           'name'                  => 'Dennis',
5           'style'         => 'Fedora'
6   );
7
8   $user = User::find(1);
9
10  $user->hats()->insert($hat);
```

But what if the objects already exist, and we just want to create the relationship between them? We can do this easily with the attach() method by passing the $id (or the object) of the object to be related. Let's see the code.

```php
1   <?php
2
3   $user->hats()->attach($hat_id);
```

The pivot will have been updated for you!

Next is a method that I myself have only recently become aware of. I will assume it arrived with Eloquent in 3.1. We can use the sync() method with an array of ids and once the method has executed only the id's in the array will be in the pivot table. Very handy! Here's a code snippet.

```php
1  <?php
2
3  $user->hats()->sync(array(4, 7, 8));
```

11.4 Pivot Tables

What if we want access to our pivot table directly, rather than just the tables that are related? Eloquent provides the pivot() method to accomplish this task.

```php
1  <?php
2
3  $pivot = $user->hats()->pivot();
```

Now we have an array of result objects, just like any other query, but for those which relate the users hats.

What if we want to retrieve the exact row that has been used to relate an object? This is easy with the pivot dynamic attribute. The official docs has a great example of this, and I am going to steal it because I am a nasty person. Don't worry, I will make it look a bit different. Kinda like with your high school assignments?

```php
1  <?php
2
3  $user = User::find(1);
4
5  foreach ($user->hats as $hat)
6  {
7          echo $hat->pivot->created_at;
8  }
```

Now we can access the created_at field on the pivot table row to see when our hat was made.

Ok, I'm getting pretty sick of hats! In fact I want to delete my hats, every last one of them. Fortunately I know my user id, its number 7, lucky number 7. Let's do it right now, let's delete() all of my hats!

```php
1  <?php
2
3  User::find(7)->hats()->delete();
```

There done. I will have a cold head from now on, but its worth it now you know how to use the delete() method.

11.5 Eager Loading

Eloquent gives the option of Eager Loading to help solve the highly debated N+1 issue. If you don't know what this is, let me break it down for you using what we have already learned. Take a look at the following snippet of code.

```php
<?php

$users = User::all();

foreach ($users as $user)
{
        echo $user->hat->size();
}
```

For every loop iteration, Eloquent has to perform another SQL query to retrieve that users Hat object and find its size. Now this isn't going to be a huge problem on small data sets, but with hundreds of rows it could drastically affect performance. With eager loading we can tell Eloquent to run a SELECT * FROM hats; when retrieving the User object so that we already have all the data we need. This reduces the amount of strain to only two SQL queries. Much better!

Let's see how we can tell Eloquent to eager load a relation:

```php
<?php

$users = User::with('hat')->get();
```

There, now the hat relationship is eager loaded. If we want to eager load several relationships, simply pass an array to the with() method. It's worth noting that the with() method is static and as such must always be at the start of the chain.

You can even eager load nested relationships. Let's assume that our Hat object has a hatstand() relationship to let us know which stand it's on. We can eager load both of the relationships like this.

```php
<?php

$users = User::with(array('hat', 'hat.hatstand'))->get();
```

Simply prefix the relationship name with the nested object.

What if we want to add some conditions to our eager loading? Maybe we are only going to be using blue hats? Of course we can do this with Eloquent! Simply pass the relationship name as a key to the array, and a closure containing conditions as a parameter. This is better explained through code.

```php
1  <?php
2
3  $users = User::with(array('hat' => function($query) {
4          $query->where('color', '=', 'blue');
5  }))->get();
```

Simple. You can add as many queries as you need to!

11.6 Setters and Getters

Setters are handy little methods that allow us to format our new model data in a certain way when it is assigned. Let's take a look at a code snippet.

```php
1  <?php
2
3  public function set_password($password)
4  {
5      $this->set_attribute('hashed_password', Hash::make($password));
6  }
```

We create a method with the name of the setter prefixed with set_, and pass it a variable which will receive the field value. Now we can use set_attribute() to set a field to its new value. This will allow us to modify the passed value anyway we like. The snippet above will cause the hashed_password field to be updated with a hashed version of the supplied value when we call :

```php
1  <?php
2
3  $user->password = "secret_panda_ninja";
```

Very useful!

Getters are the exact opposite. They can be used to adjust a value when it is being read. For example :

```php
1  <?php
2
3  public function get_panda_name()
4  {
5      return 'Panda'.$this->get_attribute('name');
6  }
```

Now if our name is Dayle we can use..

```php
1   <?php
2
3   echo $user->panda_name;
```

which would give 'PandaDayle'.

In the next chapter we will take a look at Laravel's simple events system.

12 Events

Events are a way of letting other pieces of code extend your applications in a neat way. Some other applications refer to this type of extension as a 'Hook'. If you are a 'PHP Guru' you might see some resemblances to the 'Observer / Observable' design pattern.

Events may have any number of listeners and firing them can return a varied number of responses. I think the best way to learn will be to see this in action. Let's take a closer look at Events in Laravel.

12.1 Fire An Event

```php
<?php

$responses = Event::fire('dinner.time');
```

In this example we 'trigger', or 'fire' the event `dinner.time` which alerts all of the listeners of the event that it is time to get your grub on. The `$responses` variable will contain an array of responses that the listeners of the event will provide, more on that later.

We can also retrieve the first response from an event, rather than all of them. We simply call the `first()` method instead of `fire()` and now we receive a single result like this.

```php
<?php

$response = Event::first('dinner.time');
```

It's worth noting that although we are only receiving one response, all of the events listeners will be informed. This means that the event will be fired just as if it was using the `fire()` method, but all responses apart from the first will be ignored.

The third option for firing an event is the `until()` method. This method will fire the event, notifying each listener until the first response that is a 'NON-NULL' value is returned. The first 'NON-NULL' value is then passed to the $response variable.

```php
<?php

$response = Event::until('dinner.time');
```

Well now that we know how to fire an event, let's have a look at the other end of the spectrum. We need to know how to register ourselves as a listener. We don't want to miss our dinner!

12.2 Listen for an Event

To listen for an event we use the... yeah you probably guessed it. The listen() method. We hand it the name of the event that we are looking for as a string, and as the second parameter a closure to be performed when the event has been fired. The result of the closure will be passed back as a response. Let's take a look.

```php
1  <?php
2
3  Event::listen('dinner.time', function() {
4        return 'thanks for the grub!';
5  });
```

If we now call $val = Event::first('dinner.time'); the value of $val will be thanks for the grub!. Simple as that.

12.3 Events With Parameters

Extra information can be passed to a listener from a fired event by passing an array of values to the event closure. Like this..

```php
1  <?php
2
3  $responses = Event::fire('dinner.time', array(1, 2, 3));
```

We can then add parameters to the closure in our listener to 'catch' these values, like so :

```php
1  <?php
2
3  Event::listen('dinner.time', function($one, $two, $three) {
4        return 'thanks for the grub!';
5  });
```

Easy as pie! Which coincidentally is what is for dinner.

12.4 Laravel Events

Here are the events that can be found inside the Laravel core. Normally you won't have to interact with these, but once you have become a Laravel Guru you may feel the need to bend the framework to your will. Using these events is one such example of doing so.

```php
1  <?php
2
3  Event::listen('laravel.log', function($type, $message){});
```

A new laravel log entry has been created.

```php
1  <?php
2
3  Event::listen('laravel.query', function($sql, $bindings, $time){});
```

An SQL query has been performed.

```php
1  <?php
2
3  Event::listen('laravel.done', function($response){});
```

Laravel's work is done, and the response is ready to be sent.

```php
1  <?php
2
3  Event::listen('404', function(){});
```

A page could not be found.

and many more.

> *Note:* It is best to prefix your event with the application name to avoid conflicts with other events. This is why all Laravel events start with `laravel..`

12.5 Example Usage

So where will using Events come in handy? Well imagine we have a simple task management application. These types of applications will likely have a `User` type object to allow our users to login and use the application. `User` objects can also be created to add more users to the system. Let's attach a Laravel Event to the user creation process..

```php
1  <?php
2
3  $new_user = array(.. user details here ..);
4  $u = new User($new_user);
5  $u->save();
6
7  Event::fire('myapp.new_user', array($u->id));
```

As you can see, we pass the new user's id value to the 'myapp.new_user' event so that all event listeners are aware of which user has been created.

Now let's create an extension to our application. The extension should not interfere with the existing code of the application, it could be an extra library, or a bundle, anything outside of the main application.

In our extension we are going to add a prefix to the users name (this is somehow useful to our extension). Let's do this by listening to the user event.

```php
<?php

Event::listen('myapp.new_user', function ($uid) {
        $user = User::find($uid);
        $user->name = 'Myapp_'.$user->name;
        $user->save();
});
```

We create a listener that receives the user id. Using this we can retrieve the new user from the database and apply the changes.

We have now added some extra functionality to the application without editing its core files. It is the responsibility of the application's author to insert Event triggers or fire() methods within area's of the application that are likely to be extended. Without these events the application's source would have to be modified.

13 Blade Templates

Laravel's Blade templating engine will allow you to use very neat looking syntax to embed PHP code within your views. It also includes a number of short-cuts that allow a cleaner use of existing Laravel features. Blade's templates are cached by default, which makes them extremely fast!

As always, let's jump right in.

13.1 The Basics

To enable Blade templating, simply name your views with the extension `.blade.php` instead of `.php`, it's as simple as that!

When using `view` files with PHP frameworks, you will often find yourself using this.

```
1   <?php echo $val; ?>
```

By enabling PHP short tags we can tidy this up a little.

```
1   <?=$val?>
```

However there is still room for improvement. Let's have a look at how Blade would handle the same echo statement.

```
1   {{ $val }}
```

Neat! The spacing between the brackets is optional, but I think it looks better with it there. You see the contents of the double curly brackets is evaluated and echoed out. You can use any PHP you want in there, for example..

```
1   {{ 5 * time() }}
```

This snippet will work just as well. You see all Blade is doing, is converting `{{ 5 * time() }}` to `<?php echo 5 * time(); ?>`. Be sure to consider this if you run into any problems with blade!

13.2 Logic

What about `foreach()` loops? I use loads of them! I use a lot of `if` and `else` too. Blade simplifies all of these conditional statements through the use of the magical `@` sign, let's take a look.

```
1  <?php
2
3  @foreach ($users as $user)
4          <div class="user">{{ $user->name }}</div>
5  @endforeach
```

There, not only cleaner looking than all of those ugly PHP tags, but a lot quicker to write! What about ifs and elseifs? Well if you are used to PHP alternate syntax you will be able to guess the result. Simply replace the <?php with @ and skip the ' : ?>' all together! What we have left is..

```
1  @if ($user->name == 'Dave')
2          <p>Welcome Dave!</p>
3  @else
4          <p>Welcome Guest!</p>
5  @endif
```

Very simple! Here are the other operators you can use with Blade, they should look familiar :

```
1  <?php
2
3  @for ($i =0; $i < 100 - 1; $i++)
4      Number {{ $i }}<br />
5  @endfor
```

a standard for loop and..

```
1  <?php
2
3  @forelse ($users as $user)
4      {{ $user->name }}
5  @empty
6      <p>There are no users.</p>
7  @endforelse
```

That last one is a little special. The forelse() statement acts as a foreach() loop, but with an extra @empty which will output the result below if the supplied array is empty (has no length). This is very handy since it avoids the need for adding an extra if statement.

13.3 Blade Layouts

Blade offers another method of writing complex or nested layouts. Using its clean syntax, this could well be the best layout implementation available within the framework. You simply have to use it to understand its beauty. Let's have a look at our primary template, which is a blade view (in this case named template.blade.php) like any other.

```
1   <!DOCTYPE HTML>
2   <html lang="en-GB">
3   <head>
4           <meta charset="UTF-8">
5           <title>@yield('title')</title>
6   </head>
7   <body>
8           <div class="header">
9                   <ul>
10                  @section('navigation')
11                          <li><a href="#">Home</a></li>
12                          <li><a href="#">Blog</a></li>
13                  @yield_section
14                  </ul>
15          </div>
16
17          @yield('content')
18
19  </body>
20  </html>
```

Our main template uses the `@yield()` method to define a content region that can be filled by a view that uses this layout. Simply pass a string to the method to provide a nickname for that content region, it will then be used to identify it later.

The `@section()` and `@yield_section` are used to define a content region that will contains some default data that could be replaced at a later date. Let's have a look at a view (`page.blade.php`) that makes use of the template we have just created.

```
1   @layout('template')
2
3   @section('title')
4   Dayle's Webpage!
5   @endsection
6
7   @section('navigation')
8           @parent
9           <li><a href="#">About</a></li>
10  @endsection
11
12  @section('content')
13          <h1>Welcome!</h1>
14          <p>Welcome to Dayle's web page!</p>
15  @endsection
```

In this view we use the `@layout()` method to specify that we want to use a view named `template` that we created earlier as our layout. Now we can use `@section()` and `@endsection` to replace yielded content regions with the code found between these two methods.

In the case of the `navigation` section you will notice that we have a `@parent` stub inside the content area. Blade will replace this with the content from the base template.

If we return..

```
1  return View::make('page');
```

From our route/action we can now see our page, wrapped within the `layout` template, like so..

```
1   <!DOCTYPE HTML>
2   <html lang="en-GB">
3   <head>
4           <meta charset="UTF-8">
5           <title>Dayle's Webpage!</title>
6   </head>
7   <body>
8           <div class="header">
9                   <ul>
10                          <li><a href="#">Home</a></li>
11                          <li><a href="#">Blog</a></li>
12                          <li><a href="#">About</a></li>
13                  </ul>
14          </div>
15
16          <h1>Welcome!</h1>
17          <p>Welcome to Dayle's web page!</p>
18
19  </body>
20  </html>
```

Great! We can also use as many templates as we want to, they are simply normal Blade views!

What if we want to provide the `@section` contents from our Action/Route? Simply call the `Section::inject()` method with the section name, and a string representing the sections contents, for it to be injected into the view.

```
1  Route::get('/', array('do' => function()
2  {
3          Section::inject('title', 'My Site');
4
5          return View::make('page');
6  }));
```

and that's all! Now you can use Blade to make your views look clean and efficient, your designer will love you for it.

14 Authentication

Many applications will want a layer of Authentication. If you are writing a blog, you don't want your readers to be able to post new topics. If you're working with some sensitive data, you don't want unauthorised users accessing it.

Fortunately, Laravel has a simple, secure, and highly customisable Authentication class. Let's take a look at how we can interact with it.

14.1 Setup

Before we begin you are going to need to create a new table to store our user details. We can name this table whatever we like, but if we name it users we won't have to change the Authentication's configuration file. Here's how to create a suitable table with the Schema Builder.

```php
1   <?php
2
3   Schema::create('users', function($table) {
4           $table->increments('id');
5           $table->string('username', 128);
6           $table->string('password', 64);
7   });
```

You can add as many additional fields as you like, but this will get us going. Let's also create a sample user that we can use to test the authentication process. First I should explain how the Hash class works.

You can use the Hash class to hash a password using the highly secure bcrypt algorithm. It's very simple to use, here is an example.

```php
1   <?php
2
3   $pass = Hash::make('my_password_string');
```

In the above snippet we create a bcrypt hash out of our password. By storing the hash in the database instead of the plain text password, it offers our users some extra security. You will find this is common practice with web applications.

If you would like to compare a hashed password with a value, simply use the check() method. For example..

```php
1   <?php
2
3   Hash::check('my_pass', $pass);
```

This will return a boolean result true on successful match, and false on failure. Now that we know how to hash a password, we can create our sample user. I am going to call him Dexter. You see I am watching the TV show Dexter while writing this chapter, it's great to write with background noise, try it with coding, it really works! Onwards to Dexter..

```php
<?php

DB::table('users')->insert(array(
        'username'          => 'Dexter',
        'password'          => Hash::make('knife')
));
```

Now we must choose which of the default authentication drivers we wish to use. We have the choice of 'eloquent' or 'fluent'.

The 'fluent' driver will use Fluent to interact with the database, and return an object representing the the user tables row when we call Auth::user(). The eloquent driver will return an Eloquent model representing the user instead.

Configuration for authentication driver, table or object name, and field names can all be found within 'application/config/auth.php'.

```php
<?php

return array(

        'driver' => 'eloquent',

        'username' => 'email',

        'model' => 'User',

        'table' => 'users',
);
```

Let's change 'driver' to fluent to use the fluent query builder as the authentication driver, and change the 'username' config item to 'username' so that we can log our users into our application using their username rather than an email address.

```php
<?php

return array(

        'driver' => 'fluent',

        'username' => 'username',
```

```
 8
 9            'model' => 'User',
10
11            'table' => 'users',
12    );
```

14.2 Setting up the form

Righto! We are going to need a login form, let's make a pretty one with blade! We love Blade now right? Let's do it. Creating `login.blade.php`..

```
 1    {{ Form::open('login') }}
 2    /
 3            <!-- check for login errors flash var -->
 4            @if (Session::has('login_errors'))
 5                    <span class="error">Username or password incorrect.</span>
 6            @endif
 7
 8            <!-- username field -->
 9            <p>{{ Form::label('username', 'Username') }}</p>
10            <p>{{ Form::text('username') }}</p>
11
12            <!-- password field -->
13            <p>{{ Form::label('password', 'Password') }}</p>
14            <p>{{ Form::password('password') }}</p>
15
16            <!-- submit button -->
17            <p>{{ Form::submit('Login') }}</p>
18
19    {{ Form::close() }}
```

That is a beautif..

Ssssh, that was a few chapters ago now, I'm not into brain washing, you can let it go. Sure is a beautiful form though! Let's create a nice route to show the form.

```
 1    <?php
 2
 3    Route::get('login', function() {
 4            return View::make('login');
 5    });
```

Let's make a POST variant of this route, we can use that to handle when the login form is submitted. That way we can use a single URL for both.

```php
1   <?php
2
3   Route::post('login', function() {
4           return 'login form sent';
5   });
```

Right let's make sure our routes work fine, actually I am pretty sure they will, but this is just a habit of mine. If we visit 'http://localhost/login' and enter some phoney data and submit the form we should get login form sent.

14.3 Handling Login

Note that before we can login, we will need to setup a session driver. This is because Laravel logins are stored in the session. If you head over to application/config/session.php it will list all your options, go ahead and choose a suitable one.

Great! Let's handle that login attempt and go to work on that post route. First let's get the input data that has been posted from the form.

```php
1    <?php
2
3    Route::post('login', function() {
4
5        // get POST data
6        $userdata = array(
7                'username'              => Input::get('username'),
8                'password'              => Input::get('password')
9        );
10
11   });
```

Sweet! We have post data, lets put it to use. We will use the Auth::attempt() method to check if the username and password can be used to login. The great thing about this method is on success it will automatically create our 'logged-in' session for us! Mucho conveniento! (I never took Spanish, sorry.).

```php
1    <?php
2
3    Route::post('login', function() {
4
5        // get POST data
6        $userdata = array(
7                'username'              => Input::get('username'),
8                'password'              => Input::get('password')
9        );
```

```
10
11          if ( Auth::attempt($userdata) )
12          {
13                  // we are now logged in, go to home
14                  return Redirect::to('home');
15          }
16          else
17          {
18                  // auth failure! lets go back to the login
19                  return Redirect::to('login')
20                          ->with('login_errors', true);
21                  // pass any error notification you want
22                  // i like to do it this way :)
23          }
24
25   });
```

If our authentication is successful, the login session is created and we are redirected to the home route. Perfect, but before we go any further let's create a logout route so that we can logout to perform future testing.

```
1    <?php
```

Route::get('logout', function() {

```
1           Auth::logout();
2           return Redirect::to('login');
3    });
```

Here we use the Auth::logout() method to destroy the login session, and head back to the login page. We are now logged out.

Right, now that we have our login working perfectly let's create our super secret home page, add a logout link, and welcome our currently logged in user.

```
1    <?php
2
3    //---- THE ROUTE ----
4
5    Route::get('home', function() {
6           return View::make('home');
7    });
8
9    //---- THE VIEW (home.blade.php) ----
10
```

```
11   <div class="header">
12           Welcome back, {{ Auth::user()->username }}!<br />
13           {{ HTML::link('logout', 'Logout') }}
14   </div>
15
16   <div class="content">
17           <h1>Squirrel Info</h1>
18           <p>This is our super red squirrel information page.</p>
19           <p>Be careful, the grey squirrels are watching.</p>
20   </div>
```

Now you can test our login loop.. Login, be greeted with the welcome page, logout. Repeat. Do this at least 800 times to set your mind to rest. Don't worry, this is normal behaviour, besides.. you get paid by the hour right PHP Guru?

You will notice that we use Auth::user() in the above example, this will return a Fluent database result object representing the current logged in user. Very handy for finding its id, or echoing out welcome information.

14.4 Protecting Routes

Ok, we are almost done here! There is a slight bug, a security issue that we need to take care of first. Logout of the system, (no not the machine you are reading this on, just the site) and head over to the home URL by hand.

Uh oh, now the grey squirrels can see our attack plans without even logging in! We will need to fix this. Also because we don't have a user logged into the system, we get an undefined index (or something similar) error when trying to access the user's username.

Cast your mind way back, the solution is there lurking in the shadows near the start of the book. What? No shadows? I paid the publisher to put them in... never mind let's carry on. Do you remember route filters? Using filters we can run a snippet of code before the route is executed, and if we return something it will be used in place of what we return from our route. Woah, lots of potential there.

It's even easier than that, you see Taylor has a degree in amateur mind reading, he knew we would be writing this chapter, and he knew we would need to protect a route from non-logged in users. That is why he created the 'auth' filter, which is included with Laravel as standard. Let's have a look at the filter itself. (You can find this in routes.php)

```
1    <?php
2
3    Route::filter('auth', function()
4    {
5            if (Auth::guest()) return Redirect::to('login');
6    });
```

Neat!

You see the `Auth::guest()` method? It's a nicely expressive method which returns true only if the current request has no logged in user. Very handy! You can also use `Auth::check()` to perform the opposite check, to see if a user is currently logged in. We know these methods do exactly the same thing, but by providing clean expressive method names, using the right one will appear much clearer within your source.

As you can see, if no user is logged in the `auth` filter returns a redirect to the login page, overwriting the view supplied by our route. All we need to do is attach this to our `home` route.

```
1   <?php
2
3   Route::get('home', array('before' => 'auth', 'do' => function() {
4         return View::make('home');
5   }));
```

There we go, now the home route is protected, the `undefined` notices will never be seen, and unauthorised squirr... users will no longer be able to see the home page. Please remember not to apply the `auth` filter to your `login` URI, you will experience a terrible loop!

14.5 Customisation

I know what you're thinking. What if I don't want to use Eloquent or Fluent, this seems very limited!

Please, this is Laravel. You should have learned this by now! Laravel allows you to create custom classes known as 'Auth Drivers' so that you can modify parameters or hook into any authentication system you like. Simply create a new class. I like to put mine in `application/libraries` so that they are auto-loaded for me!

```
1    <?php
2
3    // application/libraries/myauth.php
4    class Myauth extends Laravel\Auth\Drivers\Driver {
5
6          public function attempt($arguments = array())
7          {
8
9          }
10
11         public function retrieve($id)
12         {
13
14         }
15
16   }
```

Your authentication driver must extend `Laravel\Auth\Drivers\Driver` and contain the two methods listed above. The first method accepts the array of `username` and `password` and is used to authenticate using your own method. On a successful authentication you should make a call to the `login()` method of the parent to inform Laravel that the authentication worked, for example..

```php
<?php

public function attempt($arguments = array())
{
        $username = $arguments['username'];
        $password = $arguments['password'];

        $result = my_login_method($username, $password);

        if($result)
        {
                return $this->login($result->id, array_get($arguments, 'remember'));
        }

        return false;
}
```

The login method accepts an identifier (that can be used later to retrieve the user) and the value of the 'remember' key from our arguments array. On authentication failure the method should always return false.

The `retrieve()` method is handed the identifier that you previously passed to the `login()` method, you can use this to return an object that represents the current user. For example..

```php
<?php

public function retrieve($id)
{
        return get_my_user_object($id);
}
```

Great! Now we have a working authentication driver. Before we can use it we will need to register it with the `Auth` class. Add the following code to your `application/start.php`.

```php
<?php

Auth::extend('myauth', function() {
        return new Myauth();
});
```

Pass an identifier for your authentication driver as the first parameter to `Auth::extend()`, the second parameter is a Closure that is used to return a new instance of the class.

All that is left to do is update your `application/config/auth.php` file to point to this new authentication driver..

```php
1   <?php
2
3   'driver' => 'myauth',
```

and now enjoy using your authentication system in the usual way!

15 The Blog Tutorial

It's finally time to write our first full application. If you haven't read the other chapters you might find this a little tricky. Let's have a look at what we are going to be using to create the blog.

- Routes

- Migrations

- Eloquent

- Blade Templates

- Authentication

- Filters

Let's have a look at the plan Stan, and see exactly what we are going to be building.

Oh yeah, if you would like to see what we are making then you will find the source code for this tutorial on github[1].

15.1 The Design

We are going to build a three page blog. The first page will consist of a listing of blog posts. Similar to the front of a Wordpre.. Wordpush blog. The next page will be the `full-view` page. It is the page you reach when you click an article that you want to read. The final page will be the page where we write our posts.

Normally you would have the ability to edit or delete posts, but we can add all that stuff later. I'm not counting the usual login page in that count, since it is used with any application that implements authentication.

Let's think about the database schema for a moment. We know that we are going to need a table to store our blog posts. We will also need a table to store our users. We are also going to need some form of relationship between them both. Let's map this out and think about the fields.

`Table : posts`

Field	Type
id	INTEGER
title	VARCHAR(128)
body	TEXT
author_id	INTEGER
created_at	DATETIME
updated_at	DATETIME

---

[1]https://github.com/codehappy/blog-tutorial-code

```
Table : users
```

Field	Type
id	INTEGER
username	VARCHAR(128)
nickname	VARCHAR(128)
password	VARCHAR(64)
created_at	DATETIME
updated_at	DATETIME

Ok that looks good. We can use the `author_id` field on the `Post` object to reference the `User` object, which represents the post's author.

Right, to work!

15.2 Basic Setup

First of all you will need to setup your database and session driver, you should know how to do this by now. I will be using mySQL as my database as always.

Now let's create migrations for our tables, again using Artisan as we did in the migrations chapter.

```
1   php artisan migrate:make create_users
```

Now our schema for `up()` along with default user account.

```php
1   <?php
2
3   Schema::create('users', function($table) {
4           $table->increments('id');
5           $table->string('username', 128);
6           $table->string('nickname', 128);
7           $table->string('password', 64);
8           $table->timestamps();
9   });
10
11  DB::table('users')->insert(array(
12          'username'           => 'admin',
13          'nickname'           => 'Admin',
14          'password'           => Hash::make('password')
15  ));
```

and let's update our `down()` method just in case.

```
1  <?php
2
3  Schema::drop('users');
```

Let's also create our posts migration. I bet you didn't see that coming?

```
1  php artisan migrate:make create_posts
```

The schema for up..

```
1  <?php
2
3  Schema::create('posts', function($table) {
4          $table->increments('id');
5          $table->string('title', 128);
6          $table->text('body');
7          $table->integer('author_id');
8          $table->timestamps();
9  });
```

and let's tear down this table in down() too.

```
1  <?php
2
3  Schema::drop('posts');
```

Let's run our migrations and get those tables in place.

```
1  php artisan migrate:install
2  php artisan migrate
```

Finally let's update our authentication configuration in application/config/auth.php to use fluent as an authentication driver, and username as a login identifier.

```
1  <?php
2
3  return array(
4
5          'driver' => 'fluent',
6          'username' => 'username',
7          'model' => 'User',
8          'table' => 'users',
9  );
```

There, now we are ready to create our Eloquent models.

15.3 Eloquent Models

Right, you know exactly how to create Eloquent models, so let's just have a look at the source.

```php
1   <?php
2
3   class User extends Eloquent
4   {
5           public function posts()
6           {
7                   return $this->has_many('Post');
8           }
9   }
10
11  class Post extends Eloquent
12  {
13          public function author()
14          {
15                  return $this->belongs_to('User', 'author_id');
16          }
17  }
```

Nice and simple, we have our User object which has_many posts, and our Post object which belongs_to a user.

15.4 Routes

Ok, we have our tables, we have models, and since we are now following my workflow let's create placeholders for the routes we will need.

```php
1   <?php
2
3   Route::get('/', function() {
4           // this is our list of posts
5   });
6
7   Route::get('view/(:num)', function($post) {
8           // this is our single view
9   });
10
11  Route::get('admin', function() {
12          // show the create new post form
13  });
14
```

```
15   Route::post('admin', function() {
16           // handle the create new post form
17   });
18
19   Route::get('login', function() {
20           // show the login form
21   });
22
23   Route::post('login', function() {
24           // handle the login form
25   });
26
27   Route::get('logout', function() {
28           // logout from the system
29   });
```

Right, those are done. As you can see I am using GET and POST to show and handle forms with the same URI.

15.5 Views

Let's start by creating a blade layout as a wrapper for our application.

templates/main.blade.php

```
1    <!DOCTYPE HTML>
2    <html lang="en-GB">
3    <head>
4            <meta charset="UTF-8">
5            <title>Wordpush</title>
6            {{ HTML::style('css/style.css') }}
7    </head>
8    <body>
9            <div class="header">
10                   <h1>Wordpush</h1>
11                   <h2>Code is Limmericks</h2>
12           </div>
13
14           <div class="content">
15                   @yield('content')
16           </div>
17   </body>
18   </html>
```

As you can see we have a very simple HTML5 template, with a CSS style-sheet (which we will not be covering, by all means use it to make your blog pretty.. but this is not a design book) and a yielded content area for our page content.

We are going to need a login form so that our post authors can create new entries. I am going to steal this view from the last tutorial and hack it a bit to work with blade layouts. This is actually good practice. Re-use anything you can and eventually you will have built up your own Laravel development toolkit.

pages/login.blade.php

```
1   @layout('templates.main')
2
3   @section('content')
4           {{ Form::open('login') }}
5
6                   <!-- check for login errors flash var -->
7                   @if (Session::has('login_errors'))
8                           <span class="error">Username or password incorrect.</span>
9                   @endif
10
11                  <!-- username field -->
12                  <p>{{ Form::label('username', 'Username') }}</p>
13                  <p>{{ Form::text('username') }}</p>
14
15                  <!-- password field -->
16                  <p>{{ Form::label('password', 'Password') }}</p>
17                  <p>{{ Form::password('password') }}</p>
18
19                  <!-- submit button -->
20                  <p>{{ Form::submit('Login') }}</p>
21
22          {{ Form::close() }}
23  @endsection
```

As you can see, our login form is using our newly created blade layout. Let's also create our 'Create New Post' form.

pages/new.blade.php

```
1   <?php
2
3   @layout('templates.main')
4
5   @section('content')
6           {{ Form::open('admin') }}
7
8                   <!-- title field -->
9                   <p>{{ Form::label('title', 'Title') }}</p>
10                  {{ $errors->first('title', '<p class="error">:message</p>') }}
11                  <p>{{ Form::text('title', Input::old('title')) }}</p>
```

```
12
13                  <!-- body field -->
14                  <p>{{ Form::label('body', 'Body') }}</p>
15                  {{ $errors->first('body', '<p class="error">:message</p>') }}
16                  <p>{{ Form::textarea('body', Input::old('body')) }}</p>
17
18                  <!-- submit button -->
19                  <p>{{ Form::submit('Create') }}</p>
20
21          {{ Form::close() }}
22  @endsection
```

15.6 Get Coding

Finally it's time to get our hands dirty! Let's start with the authentication routine. First we need
to link our login route to the login form view.

```
1   <?php
2
3   Route::get('login', function() {
4           return View::make('pages.login');
5   });
```

There, that wasn't so hard. Now let's handle the authentication in the POST route in the usual
way.

```
1   <?php
2
3   Route::post('login', function() {
4
5       $userdata = array(
6               'username' => Input::get('username'),
7               'password' => Input::get('password')
8       );
9
10      if ( Auth::attempt($userdata) )
11      {
12              return Redirect::to('admin');
13      }
14      else
15      {
16              return Redirect::to('login')
17                      ->with('login_errors', true);
18      }
19  });
```

Now we can login to our system. If you have any trouble understanding these topics please refer to the previous chapters, we aren't covering anything new here.

Let's create the logout route, so that we can test the login process.

```php
1   <?php
2
3   Route::get('logout', function() {
4           Auth::logout();
5           return Redirect::to('/');
6   });
```

Let's add a small profile section to the header of our main template. We can use this to login or logout from the system.

```
1   <div class="header">
2           @if ( Auth::guest() )
3                   {{ HTML::link('admin', 'Login') }}
4           @else
5                   {{ HTML::link('logout', 'Logout') }}
6           @endif
7           <hr />
8
9           <h1>Wordpush</h1>
10          <h2>Code is Limmericks</h2>
11  </div>
```

Now to add the auth filter to both admin routes. You will notice that admin is the only route that needs protecting, since we want people to be able to browse our blog but not write anything.

```php
1   <?php
2
3   Route::get('admin', array('before' => 'auth', 'do' => function() {
4           // show the create new post form
5   }));
6
7   Route::post('admin', array('before' => 'auth', 'do' => function() {
8           // handle the create new post form
9   }));
```

Let's also attach the create new post form to the admin GET route while we are here. We should also hand the currently logged in user to this view. That way we can use the user objects id field to identify the author.

```php
1   <?php
2
3   Route::get('admin', array('before' => 'auth', 'do' => function() {
4           $user = Auth::user();
5           return View::make('pages.new')->with('user', $user);
6   }));
```

Now that we have a handle on our currently logged in user, let's add that information to the create new post view to identify our author. A hidden field should do the trick.

```php
1   <?php
2
3   ...
4
5   {{ Form::open('login') }}
6
7           <!-- author -->
8           {{ Form::hidden('author_id', $user->id) }}
9
10          <!-- title field -->
11          <p>{{ Form::label('title', 'Title') }}</p>
12          <p>{{ Form::text('title') }}</p>
13
14  ...
```

We can now identify our author, and the create new post page is ready. We don't need to link to it, we want it hidden. We can simply hit the URL /admin if we want to create a new post.

Let's handle a new post creation.

```php
1   <?php
2
3   Route::post('admin', function() {
4
5           // let's get the new post from the POST data
6           // this is much safer than using mass assignment
7           $new_post = array(
8                   'title'         => Input::get('title'),
9                   'body'              => Input::get('body'),
10                  'author_id' => Input::get('author_id')
11          );
12
13          // let's setup some rules for our new data
14          // I'm sure you can come up with better ones
15          $rules = array(
16                  'title'         => 'required|min:3|max:128',
```

```
17                      'body'                   => 'required'
18              );
19
20              // make the validator
21              $v = Validator::make($new_post, $rules);
22
23              if ( $v->fails() )
24              {
25                      // redirect back to the form with
26                      // errors, input and our currently
27                      // logged in user
28                      return Redirect::to('admin')
29                                      ->with('user', Auth::user())
30                                      ->with_errors($v)
31                                      ->with_input();
32              }
33
34              // create the new post
35              $post = new Post($new_post);
36              $post->save();
37
38              // redirect to viewing our new post
39              return Redirect::to('view/'.$post->id);
40
41      });
```

Now we should be able to create some blog posts, go ahead! Write a few articles so we have something to view in our list all posts view.

Speaking of which, let's get to work on that.

```
1       <?php
2
3       Route::get('/', function() {
4               // lets get our posts and eager load the
5               // author
6               $posts = Post::with('author')->all();
7
8               return View::make('pages.home')
9                       ->with('posts', $posts);
10      });
```

We also need a view to list all of our blog posts, here we go..

pages/home.blade.php

```
1   <?php
2
3   @layout('templates.main')
4
5   @section('content')
6          @foreach ($posts as $post)
7                  <div class="post">
8                          <h1>{{ HTML::link('view/'.$post->id, $post->title) }}</h1>
9                          <p>{{ substr($post->body,0, 120).' [..]' }}</p>
10                         <p>{{ HTML::link('view/'.$post->id, 'Read more &rarr;') }}</p>
11                 </div>
12         @endforeach
13  @endsection
```

Finally we need a full view for our blog posts, let's call it..

pages/full.blade.php

```
1   <?php
2
3   @layout('templates.main')
4
5   @section('content')
6          <div class="post">
7                  <h1>{{ HTML::link('view/'.$post->id, $post->title) }}</h1>
8                  <p>{{ $post->body }}</p>
9                  <p>{{ HTML::link('/', '&larr; Back to index.') }}</p>
10         </div>
11  @endsection
```

We also need to add a new route to enable the view..

```
1   Route::get('view/(:num)', function($post) {
2          $post = Post::find($post);
3          return View::make('pages.full')
4                  ->with('post', $post);
5   });
```

Now we have a fully working blog, with just the basics. Let's take a quick look at what we could do to improve it. Go ahead and try to add some of these features to test your Laravel skills.

15.7 The Future

Pagination

We could add some pagination to the posts list page, which would come in handy when the post count gets lengthy. Laravel let's you paginate Eloquent models easily, so this should be a walk in the park!

Edit / Delete Posts

Adding the functionality to edit or remove posts wouldn't be a lot of work, and would allow for maintenance to be performed on the blog.

Post Slugs

We could create post slugs to use instead of post `ids` in our URLs, this will result in better search engine optimisation. We would need to create a slug from the post title upon saving a new article, and then detect the slug from a route parameter.

16 Unit Testing

Unit testing can be a very useful tool for a web developer. It can be used to check whether adding a feature, or modifying the codebase in some way has accidentally altered another feature, causing it to fail. Some developers even practice Test-Driven Development (TDD), where tests are written before the code to ensure that the code being written meets all requirements.

Laravel provides the `tests` directory to contain all of your applications tests, and even adds a helper command to Artisan the CLI interface for running PHPUnit test cases.

Not only can the application be tested, but bundles can also contain their own test suites. In fact Laravel has a bundle devoted to testing the core features of the framework, it can be found in the Laravel tests github repository[1].

16.1 Installation

No we're not going to cover the Laravel installation again!

Laravel uses the PHPUnit software to execute its tests, before we can use the unit testing features of Laravel we will need to install this software.

Installation of PHPUnit can vary from operating system to operating system, therefore I think it would be best to look at the official documentation for PHP Unit to find installation instructions. You will find the installation page here[2].

16.2 Creating a Test

Let's take a look at a test case, fortunately Laravel has included an example test case for us!

```php
1   <?php
2
3   // application/tests/example.test.php
4
5   class TestExample extends PHPUnit_Framework_TestCase {
6
7       /**
8        * Test that a given condition is met.
9        *
10       * @return void
11       */
12      public function testSomethingIsTrue()
13      {
14          $this->assertTrue(true);
```

---

[1]https://github.com/laravel/tests
[2]http://www.phpunit.de/manual/current/en/installation.html

98

```
15              }
16
17  }
```

As you can see we create our test cases in a file with the extension test.php, the name of the class must start with the word Test and it must extend the class PHPUnit_Framework_TestCase. These are limitations set not by Laravel, but by the PHPUnit software.

A PHPUnit test case may contain any number of tests, as camel-cased actions, prefixed with the word test. Our tests can contain a number of different assertions that decide whether our tests will pass or fail.

A full list of assertions can be found on the PHPUnit documentation website[3].

16.3 Running Tests

Tests can be ran using the Artisan command line interface. Simply use the test command to run all test cases.

```
1  php artisan test
```

and the result..

```
1  PHPUnit 3.6.10 by Sebastian Bergmann.
2
3  Configuration read from /home/daylerees/www/laravel/develop/phpunit.xml
4
5  .
6
7  Time: 0 seconds, Memory: 6.25Mb
8
9  OK (1 test, 1 assertion)
```

With the OK part appearing in bright green to show us that the tests have passed.

Of course we knew that the test would succeed because we are using the assertTrue() method to check the value true. There is no way it could fail.

Let's bully the test so that it will fail, we will simply change the parameter to false.

```
1  ...
2  $this->assertTrue(false);
3  ...
```

and the result :

---

[3]http://www.phpunit.de/manual/current/en/writing-tests-for-phpunit.html#writing-tests-for-phpunit.assertions

```
1   PHPUnit 3.6.10 by Sebastian Bergmann.
2
3   Configuration read from /home/daylerees/www/laravel/develop/phpunit.xml
4
5   F
6
7   Time: 0 seconds, Memory: 6.50Mb
8
9   There was 1 failure:
10
11  1) TestExample::testSomethingIsTrue
12  Failed asserting that false is true.
13
14  /home/daylerees/www/laravel/develop/application/tests/example.test.php:12
15  /usr/bin/phpunit:46
16
17  FAILURES!
18  Tests: 1, Assertions: 1, Failures: 1.
```

Now we have some bright red lines to indicate that the tests have failed, including some details about why the test failed.

If we wanted to test a bundle we would simply pass the bundle name as a parameter to the test command, for example.

```
1   php artisan test mybundle
```

16.4 Testing The Core

Laravel's core is well unit tested, if you would like to run the tests yourself, here is how you can do it.

Install the tests bundle

Download the tests bundle from github[4] and extract it in the bundles/laravel-tests directory. Or use php artisan bundle:install laravel-tests to achieve the same goal.

Now simply use the command test:core to execute the core test package.

```
1   php artisan test:core
```

---

[4]https://github.com/laravel/tests

17 Caching

Laravel offers a very simple to use Caching class, allowing you to easily cache anything you need to, for however long you like. Confused? Let's take a look at it in action.

17.1 Setup

There are many ways to store your cached data you must set a driver stating which storage method you want to use in `application/config/cache.php`. The options are 'file', 'memcached', 'apc', 'redis', and 'database'. You may experience better performance with 'apc' or 'memcached' but I am going to use 'file' based caching for its simplicity to setup.

```php
1  <?php
2
3  'driver' => 'file',
```

17.2 Setting values

You can use the `put()` or `forever()` methods to store data in the Cache.

The `put()` method allows you to store a value for a set period of time, let's have a look at a code sample..

```php
1  <?php
2
3  $data = 'complicated_generated_data';
4  Cache::put('mydata', $data, 10);
```

Let's pretend that `$data` wasn't just an assigned string, but the result of a complicated algorithm that would take some time to process. We don't want to process this data all the time, so we keep it in the cache.

The first parameter to the method is the key, a string used to identify the cached data. The second parameter is the data itself, and the third is the amount of time in minutes to cache to the data.

The `forever()` method takes only the first two parameters, and acts exactly as the name implies. The data is cached forever.

17.3 Retrieving Values

To retrieve an item from the cache use the `get()` method and supply the key, for example..

```php
1   <?php
2
3   $data = Cache::get('mydata');
```

By default, if the cached item does not exist or has expired already, the method will return NULL. However, you can pass an optional second parameter to provide an alternate default value.

```php
1   <?php
2
3   $data = Cache::get('mydata', 'complicated data');
```

You can also pass a closure as the second parameter and the value returned by the closure will be used if the cache data does not exist. The closure will only be executed if the key does not exist.

17.4 A better way

You might find yourself using the has() method to check if a cached item exists, and falling into this familiar pattern..

```php
1   <?php
2
3   if (! Cache::has('mydata'))
4   {
5           $data = 'complicated_generated_data';
6           Cache::put('mydata', $data, 10);
7   }
8
9   return $data;
```

However, you can use the remember() method as a much more elegant solution. The remember() method will return the value if it exists in the cache, or it will store and return the value of the second parameter for a defined length of time, for example..

```php
1   <?php
2
3   return Cache::remember('mydata', function () {
4           return 'complicated_generated_data';
5   }, 10);
```

Of course the closure will not be executed unless the key does not exist or has expired.

Have fun using the Cache!

18 Autoloading Classes

With many frameworks knowing where to put your files, and how to load class definitions can be a tricky topic. However with Laravel there are no strict rules applied to the layout of your application. Laravel's auto loader is a clever library which simplifies the loading of classes with various naming or sub-folder conventions. It is flexible enough to handle the addition of complex libraries or packages with ease. Let's have a look at the functions we have available.

18.1 Mappings

Mappings are the simplest method of loading classes, you can pass the auto loader an array of Class name to file location key-value pairs and Laravel will handle the rest. It's efficient autoloader will only load the required class definition when the class is used. By default the Autoloader mappings are set within the start.php file, you can however use the class from anywhere, but the start.php file is a good choice due to it being loaded early. Let's take a look at a mapping..

```php
1   <?php
2
3   // application/start.php
4
5   Autoloader::map(array(
6           'Cloud'                 => path('app').'libraries/ff/cloud.php',
7           'Tifa'                  => path('app').'libraries/ff/tifa.php',
8   ));
```

The path('app') is a handy helper method to retrieve the absolute path to your projects application folder. You can also retrieve absolute paths to other folders using the path() method, here is a short list.

Method	Directory
path('app')	application
path('sys')	laravel
path('bundle')	bundles
path('storage')	storage

In the mapping example, you will see that we specify our Class name as the array index, and the file and location as the value. So if we wish to use the Cloud class..

```php
1   <?php
2
3   $c = new Cloud();
```

Laravel's autoloader will 'detect' (php magic methods) that a class definition needs to be loaded, it will look at the mapping definitions to see if our Class exists there, and proceed to `include()` the source.

18.2 Directory Mapping

If you have a number of Classes which follow the Class name to lower-case file name pattern, you may want to specify the directory, rather than each file individually. You can do this by using the `directories()` method of the Autoloader, however this time you need only supply an array of values as locations and file names. For example..

```php
1   <?php
2
3   Autoloader::directories(array(
4           path('app').'smurfs'
5   ));
```

Now all of our classes inside the `application/smurfs` directory will be auto loaded, so long as their file name matches the lower-case of their Class name.

18.3 Namespace Mapping

PHP 5.3 saw the arrival of name-spacing. Although far from perfect, name-spacing allows the PSR-0 convention of loading files. Under the PSR-0, namespaces are used to indicate directory structure, and class names are used to identify the file name, therefore we can assume that..

```php
1   <?php namespace Paladin\Mage;
2
3   class Princess
4   {
5           // so pretty
6   }
```

will live in the file..

```
paladin/mage/princess.php
```

Before we can use this convention, Laravel needs to know where our root namespace directory is. We can help it find our files by using the `namespaces()` method of the `Autoloader` class, for example..

```php
1   <?php
2
3   Autoloader::namespaces(array(
4           'Paladin'          => path('libraries').'paladin'
5   ));
```

As you can see we pass an array to the method. The array key represents the name of the root namespace, in this case `Paladin` and the and array value is used to indicate the root folder that is matched by this namespace, in my example `application/libraries/paladin`.

18.4 Mapping Underscores

Well we don't actually need to map the underscore, it's sitting right there on the keyboard, always watching, judging... Look I'm sorry underscore, I may abuse you a little but it's purely out of love. Camel-casing simply looks wrong to me!

Sorry about that outburst, we will discuss it later in private. The reason that the title is named mapping underscores is because in 'ye olde' days of PHP, before namespaces (and Laravel) had arrived many developers chose to use underscores within file names to separate sub directories. Laravel offers the `underscored` method on the Autoloader to accommodate this type of class loading. Once more pass an array with the key representing the class prefix and the value representing the root directory, for example..

```php
<?php

Autoloader::underscored(array(
        'Paladin'           => path('app').'jobs/pld'
));
```

and now the Class `Paladin_Light_Knight` will have its definition loaded from the file `application/jobs/pld/light/knight.php`.

So now that you know how to auto load your classes with Laravel, you will no longer have to plaster your source code with `include()` statements!

19 Configuration

Laravel has many configuration files in application/config to tweak almost every feature that the framework offers. Wouldn't it be great if you could create your own configuration files this way? Well today is your lucky day, because you can!

19.1 Creating new Configuration Files

Laravel config files are simply PHP files that live in application/config or a subdirectory, and return a PHP array. For example..

```php
1   <?php
2
3   // application/config/ourconfig.php
4
5   return array(
6
7           'size'          => 6,
8
9           'eat'           => true,
10  );
```

You can use comments to make your config files more descriptive, I like to use the style of the comments Laravel provides, for example..

```php
1   <?php
2
3   // application/config/ourconfig.php
4
5   return array(
6
7           /*
8           |-----------------------------
9           | Size
10          |-----------------------------
11          |
12          | This is the size of my thing.
13          |
14          */
15
16          'size'          => 6,
17  );
```

I'm sure you can come up with a better description! You will have noticed by now that Laravel configuration files are key-value pairs, with the array index representing the key, and the value... its value.

The value of the setting can be any value or object that PHP supports, it can even be a closure. By providing a closure you are making it easy for the user to change the configuration to enable it to be loaded from another source, for example..

```php
1   <?php
2
3   // application/config/ourconfig.php
4
5   return array(
6
7           /*
8           |-----------------------------
9           | Size
10          |-----------------------------
11          |
12          | This is the size of my thing.
13          |
14          */
15
16          'size'          => function() {
17                  $size = file_get_contents('path/to/file.json');
18                  $size = json_decode($size);
19                  return $size;
20          },
21  );
```

Now our 'size' configuration is read from the JSON contents of a file, simple!

19.2 Reading Configuration

We can read a configuration setting using the get() method..

```php
1   <?php
2
3   $option = Config::get('ourconfig.size');
```

Simply pass a string to the method, with the name of the file a period (.) and the name of the configuration key. The value will be returned. If your configuration file is in a subdirectory you will need to use extra periods to indicate the subdirectories, for example..

```
1    <?php
2
3    $option = Config::get('ourconfig.sub.directory.size');
```

Sometimes it's useful to retrieve the entire configuration array, to do this simply specify the filename without the option. To retrieve the entire configuration array from our file we would use.

```
1    <?php
2
3    $option = Config::get('ourconfig');
```

19.3 Setting Configuration

To set a configuration item, use the set() method. The first parameter represents the file and configuration item name, in the same format as the get() method. The second parameter is the value you wish to set.

```
1    <?php
2
3    Config::set('ourconfig.size', 7);
```

If a configuration item exists within a configuration file, it will be written in the runtime configuration when you use set(), however it will not be overwritten in the configuration file itself. If a configuration item doesn't exist, a call to the set() method will create it, but again not within the configuration file.

Try to put as many configurable settings as possible from your application into configuration files, it will make it much easier to configure if you have to move or redistribute the application.

20 The IoC Container

The IoC container is a tricky subject, many people are confused by its description in the documentation, and for a short time I was included in those people. A great deal of research, and the support of the fantastic Laravel community (join us in #laravel on freenode IRC) has cleared up the topic nicely. Hopefully I will be able to shed some light on this mysterious topic.

IoC stands for Inversion of Control, I don't want to complicate things with a full description, there are many online articles which will cover the nerdier side of this topic. Instead think of the container as 'Inverting the Control' or 'Handing control back to Laravel' to resolve our objects.

That's what the container is all about, resolving objects. Other than its use for injecting dependencies for use in unit tests (we will cover this later) you can simply think of the IoC container as a 'shortcut' for resolving complex objects, or following a singleton pattern, without the usual class associated with the pattern. More on singletons later, let's have a look at registering a objects with the container.

20.1 Registering Objects

Let's use our imaginations, like the big purple dinosaur on the TV taught us. We will be imagining a class called 'Discoball' which will be used all over our application for various groovy purposes.

Unfortunately, our Discoball class requires a lot of configuration before it can be used, let's have a look at that.

```php
<?php
$db = new Discoball(Discoball::SHINY);
$db->configure_shinyness('max');
$db->spin_speed('8900rpm');
```

Woah! That's a lot of settings. Now it would soon get boring to have to instantiate and setup our discoball every time we want to use it. Let's let the IoC container instantiate it for us, and jump right in with a code sample.

I like to put this code into start.php, but you can put it anywhere you like, as long as your objects are registered before you try to resolve them.

```php
<?php

// application/start.php

IoC::register('discoball', function() {

        // instantiate our object as before
        $db = new Discoball(Discoball::SHINY);
        $db->configure_shinyness('max');
```

```
10      $db->spin_speed('8900rpm');
11
12      // hand the object as the result of the closure
13      return $db;
14  });
```

We use the `IoC::register()` method to register our object with the controller. The first parameter is a string that will be used to resolve the object later, I used the word 'discoball' as it made the most sense to me. The second parameter is a closure that we can use to instantiate our object.

Inside the closure you will see the familiar discoball configuration code, and we will return the configured discoball object from the closure.

Great! Our object is registered, and that's all there is to the Io... just kidding. Let's have a look at how we can use our registered object.

20.2 Resolving Objects

Now we have our disco ball registered, let's see how we can get it back. Let's make a call to resolve.

```
1   <?php
2   $db = IoC::resolve('discoball');
```

And that's it! Instead of creating and configuring a new instance of our discoball each time, we make a call to the `resolve()` method, passing the string that identifies the object and the IoC container will execute the closure we created in the first section, and return our instantiated and configured discoball object.

Handy, and saves many lines of code!

You can register and resolve as many objects as you want, go ahead and try it. For now lets move on to singletons.

20.3 Singletons

Resolving our discoball is useful, but what if our discoball was expensive on resources to instantiate, or should only be instantiated once? The register method will not be useful in this case, since the closure is executed with every call to `resolve()` and a new instance of the object is returned each time. This is where the singleton design pattern comes in.

The singleton design pattern involves writing your classes in a certain way, so that they can be called using a static method, and will always return the same instance of itself. This way the class is instantiated only once.

For more information on the Singleton design pattern, I would suggest a quick Google search, or check out the PHP API which has an article on the subject.

Singletons can be useful, but they require a certain class structure to be able to use them. The IoC container has a `singleton()` method which makes the process a lot more simple, and does not require any special kind of class. Let's register our discoball as a singleton instead..

```php
<?php
// application/start.php

IoC::singleton('discoball', function() {

        // instantiate our object as before
        $db = new Discoball(Discoball::SHINY);
        $db->configure_shinyness('max');
        $db->spin_speed('8900rpm');

        // hand the object as the result of the closure
        return $db;
});
```

As you can see, the process is almost identical to registering an object, except that we use the method `singleton()` which accepts the same parameters.

When we resolve our discoball, the closure will only be run the first time `resolve()` is called, the resulting object will be stored, and any future calls to the `resolve()` method will return the same object instance. For example..

```php
<?php

// closure is executed, and a discoball
// instance is returned
$db = IoC::resolve('discoball');

// the same instance of the discoball
// in the above statement is returned
$another = IoC::resolve('discoball');
```

Great! It's also worth noting that you can pass an already instantiated object as a second parameter to the `singleton()` method, and it will be returned by all future requests to `resolve()` for example..

```php
<?php

$db = new Discoball(Discoball::SHINY);
IoC::singleton('discoball', $db);
```

```
5
6  // get hold of our discoball
7  $ball = IoC::resolve('discoball');
```

21 Encryption

Sometimes you need to protect your important data. Laravel provides two different methods to help you do that. One-way and two-way encryption. Let's take a look at these methods.

21.1 One Way Encryption

One way encryption is the best way to store user passwords, or other sensitive data. One way means that your data can be converted into an encrypted string, but due to a complex algorithm with painful maths, reversing the process is not possible.

This makes storing passwords a doddle! Your customers don't have to worry about you knowing their passwords, but you are still able to compare them (by hashing the password they provide) or change the password if needed.

Note that hashing is the process of creating a hash or encrypted string from another string.

Let's take a look at how password hashing works with one way encryption.

```php
1   <?php
2
3   $pass = Input::get('password');
```

Now we have retrieved the password from our 'create user' form, but it's in plain-text! Let's hash it quickly so we can store it securely in our database.

```php
1   <?php
2
3   $pass = Hash::make($pass);
```

We have used another of Laravel's highly expressive methods, this time make()ing a new Hash. Our $pass value will now contain a bcrypt encrypted version of our password, neat!

Let's say that our user has entered their password to login, and now we need to check to see if its authentic before they can be logged into the system. We can simply compare our hash to the value stored in the database with the check() method.

```php
1   <?php
2
3   $pass = Input::get('password');
4   if ( Hash::check($pass, $user->password) )
5   {
6           // auth successful
7   }
```

The `check()` method accepts two parameters, the plain-text value provided by your user, and the hashed password that you have stored. It returns a boolean value to indicate whether the true values match or not.

What if we want to decode our data at a later date? Let's two way encrypt it.

21.2 Two Way Encryption

Two way encryption, allows you to return your encrypted data to its original form, kind of like those spy code sheets you played with when you were a kid!

The Laravel Crypter class uses AES-256 encryption which is provided by the Mcrypt PHP extension, so make sure that this PHP extension has been installed before attempting to use the class!

The Crypter class works using two simple methods, `encrypt()` and `decrypt()`, let's take a look at encrypting a string.

```php
1   <?php
2
3   $secret = Crypter::encrypt('I actually like Hello Kitty');
```

Now our dirty little secret has been AES-256 encrypted, and the result has been returned. This would be of no use if we couldn't decrypt the secret at a later date. Let's look at how you can decrypt an encrypted piece of data.

```php
1   <?php
2
3   $decrypted_secret = Crypter::decrypt($secret);
```

Easy as that! Simply hand the encrypted string to the `decrypt()` and the decrypted result is handed back.

Enjoy using the Crypter class to simulate the feeling of using your super secret decoder rings you got that one time in a cereal box!

22 AJAX Content

Modern web applications don't have the time to be waiting around for the next HTTP request. Javascript has changed the way we browse, we want our content to automatically update. We want to post information without having to reload the page.

In the Laravel IRC channel we often get asked how to use Ajax alongside Laravel, which seems confusing, because the answer is simply 'like any other HTTP request'. Let's dive right in and look at some Ajax requests using the framework. We are going to need to make some HTTP requests through Javascript, this can get ugly so I have decided to use the jQuery Javascript framework in these examples.

22.1 Page Template

We will need a view, or page template to serve with our first request, so let's put together something basic.

```
1   <!-- application/views/template.php -->
2   <!DOCTYPE HTML>
3   <html>
4   <head>
5           <meta charset="UTF-8">
6           <title>My Ajax Page</title>
7   </head>
8   <body>
9           <div id="content">
10                  <p>Hello and welcome to the site!</p>
11          </div>
12          <a href="#" id="load-content">Load Content</a>
13  </body>
14  </html>
```

There we go, now we have a content area, defined in a <DIV> element with the id of content, this is where we will load out future content. We also have a link with the id of load-content which we can use as a trigger to load our new content into the <DIV> above.

Before we can see this view, we will need to define a route to load it, I am going to make it my base route..

```
1   <?php
2
3   // application/routes.php
4   Route::get('/', function() {
5           return View::make('template');
6   });
```

Now if we visit `http://localhost` we are greeted with our site template, but clicking on the load content link isn't going to do a lot without some Javascript. Although we wouldn't need Javascript if we didn't have something to load, let's create a new route and view for content that is to be loaded into the content `<DIV>`.

First the view..

```
1  <!-- application/views/content.php -->
2  <h1>New Content</h1>
3  <p>This is our AJAX loaded content.</p>
```

and a route to serve the content, note that we aren't embedding the content within a template, if we did that the template would be repeated twice when we AJAX load our new content.

```
1  <?php
2
3  // application/routes.php
4  Route::get('content', function() {
5          return View::make('content');
6  });
```

Great so now we have our main template, and we have a secondary route with some content to load via AJAX, so let's get started with the Javascript.

22.2 The Javascript

Now I'm a PHP developer, so my Javascript skills aren't going to blow anyones minds in this chapter. If you can find a better way to perform these actions (and there are many alternatives) then go ahead and try them, I'm sure you can do better!

First let's create a new file called `script.js` and put it in `public/js` along with the latest version of jQuery which in my case is simply called `jquery.js`. Let's edit our main template to add references to these files using the `HTML::script()` method.

```
1   <!-- application/views/template.php -->
2   <!DOCTYPE HTML>
3   <html>
4   <head>
5       <meta charset="UTF-8">
6       <title>My Ajax Page</title>
7   </head>
8   <body>
9       <div id="content">
10          <p>Hello and welcome to the site!</p>
11      </div>
```

```
12        <a href="#" id="load-content">Load Content</a>
13
14        <!-- javascript files -->
15        <script type="text/javascript">var BASE = "<?php echo URL::base(); ?>";\
16    </script>
17        <?php echo HTML::script('js/jquery.js'); ?>
18        <?php echo HTML::script('js/script.js'); ?>
19    </body>
20    </html>
```

As you can see, I have referenced my Javascript files before the closing tag, so that the HTTP requests to load them don't block the page loading. This is a good practice to stick to. Let's get started and add some Javascript to our public/js/script.js file.

We also create a new BASE variable so that Javascript is aware of the base URL to our application, we will need this later to create request URLs.

```
1    // public/js/script.js
2    jQuery(document).ready(function($) {
3            // perform javascript only when the document
4            // has been fully loaded
5    });
```

Here we are using the jQuery() object to get a handle on the current document, and adding a ready() event with a closure to hold our code. By waiting for the document object to be ready() we can be sure that all DOM objects have loaded, and that the jQuery library has been loaded.

You may see other examples written like this..

```
1    // public/js/script.js
2    $(document).ready(function() {
3            // perform javascript only when the document
4            // has been fully loaded
5    });
```

This is fine, but could lead to problems if other Javascript libraries chose to use the $ object at a later date. My method uses the jQuery class, and hands the inner closure a $ which is reassigned to the jQuery object. This prevents any collisions.

Let's get started on creating a click event for our content loader link, there are many ways to do this with jQuery, I am going to use the .click() method. Here we go..

```
1    // public/js/script.js
2    $(document).ready(function() {
3
4            $('#load-content').click(function(e) {
```

```
5          e.preventDefault();
6       })
7
8   });
```

Now we have a click event defined, with a callback closure. By providing an event parameter called e to the inner closure, we can use the e.preventDefault(); method to prevent the default click action from being performed. In this case the link will not act as a hyper-link. Now we need to make another HTTP request to GET the new content, and load it into our #content area. Let's use the jQuery .get() method to perform this task.

```
1   // public/js/script.js
2   $(document).ready(function() {
3       $('#load-content').click(function(e) {
4           // prevent the links default action
5           // from firing
6           e.preventDefault();
7
8           // attempt to GET the new content
9           $.get(BASE+'content', function(data) {
10              $('#content').html(data);
11          });
12      })
13  });
```

Remember the BASE attribute we set earlier? We can use it to build our request URL, and create a callback method to catch the data that is returned. We will inject the response from our GET request into the #content element using the .html() method.

That was a lot of hard work wasn't it? Well at least now we can see our hard work in action, let's load up the application at http://localhost and click the load content link. Hopefully it worked!

So as you can see, using AJAX with Laravel is the same as using any other framework or plain PHP, just be sure you format the views for your AJAX routes in a suitable manner.

22.3 Post Data

Sometimes you need to send extra along with your requests, let's create a new POST HTTP request with jQuery to demonstrate how this can be done. First we will need a route that will respond to a POST request.

```
1   <?php
2
3   // application/routes.php
```

```
4   Route::post('content', function() {
5       // deal with the post data..
6   });
```

By using the Route::post() method instead of get() our content route will now respond to our POST request, let's get started on the Javascript.

```
1   // attempt a POST request with
2   // some additional data
3   $.post(BASE+'content', {
4           name: "Dayle",
5           age: 27
6   }, function(data) {
7           $('#content').html(data);
8   });
```

We are using the POST method to post some data to the content route, we can receive the data with Laravel in a similar manner to form processing using the Input class.

```
1   <?php
2
3   // application/routes.php
4   Route::post('content', function() {
5       echo Input::get('name');        // Dayle
6       echo Input::get('age');         // 27
7   });
```

Simple as that!

22.4 JSON Responses

When interacting with Javascript, its useful to be able to return data in JSON format, a string based array that Javascript is more familiar with.

> To return a JSON response, first we need to encode our PHP array, and then send the appropriate headers to inform the client of our JSON content type.

The above quote used to be true, but the method Response::json() was added with Laravel 3.2 which achieves the same goal.

Let's create a new route.

```
1    <?php
2
3    // application/routes.php
4    Route::get('content', function() {
5
6            // our data array, soon to be JSON
7        $data = array(
8                'name'                  => 'Dummy',
9                'size'                  => 'XL',
10               'color'          => 'Blue'
11        );
12
13        return Response::json($data);
14
15   });
```

Finally we return a response object, passing our data array to the json() method which is JSON encoded for us. We can optionally pass a different status code other than 200 as a second parameter.

22.5 Detecting an AJAX Request

Sometimes its useful to within the route whether a request has been made using AJAX. Fortunately Laravel provides a method to detect AJAX requests. Let's take a look.

```
1    <?php
2
3    // application/routes.php
4    Route::get('content', function() {
5
6            // check to see if the request is
7            // an AJAX one.
8            if (Request::ajax())
9            {
10                   // provide the ajax content
11                   return View::make('only_content');
12           }
13
14           // provide the full content
15       return View::make('content_with_layout');
16
17   });
```

The Request::ajax() returns a boolean true if the request is an AJAX request, and boolean false if not.

23 Debugging Applications

Applications written using the Laravel framework are best experienced without bugs, however we all know how easily they can arise when we have deadlines to meet, and angry bosses standing over our shoulders.

PHP itself has a number of different methods of debugging, from simple `var_dump()`s, `print_r()`s, the famous `die()` and the advanced debugging features of the PHP xdebug extension. I'm not going to cover these basic methods in detail, because this is a book about Laravel, not the basics of the PHP language. Instead let's have a look at the features that Laravel offers to help us track down those mean little bugs.

23.1 Error Handler

Laravel includes a custom error handler, which overwrites the default one liner PHP errors, and instead provides some greater detail along with a stacktrace. Let's have a look at the output from the error handler..

```
1   Unhandled Exception
2
3   Message:
4
5   View [page.panda] doesn't exist.
6   Location:
7
8   /Users/daylerees/www/panda/laravel/view.php on line 151
9   Stack Trace:
10
11  #0 /Users/daylerees/www/panda/laravel/view.php(93): Laravel\View->path('pag\
12  e.panda')
13  #1 /Users/daylerees/www/panda/laravel/view.php(199): Laravel\View->__constr\
14  uct(' page.panda ', Array)
15  #2 /Users/daylerees/www/panda/application/routes.php(35): Laravel\View::mak\
16  e(' page.panda ')
17  #3 [internal function]: {closure}()
18  #4 /Users/daylerees/www/panda/laravel/routing/route.php(163): call_user_fun\
19  c_array(Object(Closure), Array)
20  #5 /Users/daylerees/www/panda/laravel/routing/route.php(124): Laravel\Routi\
21  ng\Route->response()
22  #6 /Users/daylerees/www/panda/laravel/laravel.php(125): Laravel\Routing\Rou\
23  te->call()
24  #7 /Users/daylerees/www/panda/public/index.php(34): require('/Users/daylere\
25  e...')
26  #8 {main}
```

This is the error that is shown if a requested view doesn't exist at run time. As you can see we have an informative error message from Laravel, as well as the file in which the error was encountered, and a line number. In addition we also have a stacktrace that shows the initial error, following all the method calls through the 'View' layer all the way down to the routing system.

Most of the time you won't need the stacktrace, but it could prove useful for the more experienced developers, for example when an error occurs within a complex library.

23.2 Error Configuration

We don't always want our errors to show in this way, especially on a production site where showing a stacktrace could pose a significant security risk.

Fortunately, and as always, Laravel has made it easy for us to change the configuration for the display of errors. The configuration file for the error reporting system can be found at `application/config/error.php`. Let's have a run through the configuration options that are contained in this array.

```
1   'ignore' => array(),
```

The ignore array contains a list of errors that are to be ignored by the error handler. Although these errors will no longer be displayed when they are encountered, they will always be logged. Keep this in mind when using the ignore array.

To add an error type to this array, add the PHP error type constant, or an integer value to the array.

```
1   'ignore' => array(E_ERROR);
```

A full list of PHP error type constants can be found on the PHP API, however here are some of the more useful ones.

E_ERROR This will match all fatal run time errors.

E_WARNING This constant will match all warning, or non fatal type errors.

E_PARSE This constant will match all parse time errors, or syntax errors.

E_NOTICE This constant will match all run time notices.

E_ALL This constant will match all of the above, except for E_STRICT errors.

```
1   'detail' => true,
```

The detail config option can be used to switch the detailed error reporting on or off. When enabled (true) it will show the full error report along with stack trace as shown above. Disabling this option (false) will cause the default error 500 page to be displayed instead.

```
1  'log' => false,
```

If the log config option is set to true, the closure contained within the logger config option will be executed with each error, and passed an exception object.

```
1  'logger' => function($exception)
2  {
3          Log::exception($exception);
4  },
```

By default, the closure contained within the logger config option will write an entry to a log file within the storage/logs. However, providing a closure has provided a great deal of flexibility, allowing you to override the default logging method with anything you can think of. Perhaps you would prefer to log to a database? Make it so number 1! Engage.

23.3 Logging

Being able to show errors, and log them to files is handy, but what if we want to log our own custom information? The Laravel Log class contains two different methods for logging useful information from your application. Let's take a look at these methods now.

The Log::write() method accepts a log type, and a string message to be written to the log file. For example..

```
1  <?php
2
3  Log::write('myapp', 'Here is some useful information.');
```

Will result in the following line being written to the log file.

```
1  2012-05-29 19:10:17 MYAPP - Here is some useful information.
```

The entry will of course be written to the active log file in the storage/logs directory in a file named after the current day, for example 2011-02-05.log. This allows for the logs to be rotated and avoid having log files that are huge!

You can also use a magic method to set the log type, for example..

```
1  <?php
2
3  Log::shoe('my log entry');
```

Will have the same effect as..

```php
1   <?php
2
3   Log::write('shoe', 'my log entry');
```

Very useful!

Make use of all of the features you have learned in this chapter to diagnose your applications if anything goes wrong!

24 Thanks!

In this chapter I would like to say thanks to everyone who bought the eBook. Without their support and feedback I would never have been able to publish a print version. Code Happy was a long and difficult journey for a simple programmer, and I hope the result was worth it!

Go forth, build great applications, and most of all.. Code Happy!

Thanks so much!

24.1 Payments over $19.99

We at @HelpSpot really support what you're doing to expand the Laravel community, keep up the great work! - Ian Landsman

Thanks Ian! We the Laravel community really support what you're doing to expand the Framework, so now we are even! For those of you who do not know, Ian Landsman is the head of UserScape, a company which provided the framework's author with a job that lets him expand the framework. UserScape also sponsor the bundle site for Laravel, and many other things! Please check out their product Helpspot, a wonderfully flexible and affordable piece of help desk software[1]!

Please don't forget to talk about the IoC container and how this can be useful with unit tests. You made a great choice with Laravel. - Jorge Martinez

Hey Dayle, thanks a lot for this book, the Laravel framework is just awesome ! If any french guys read this, visit http://www.laravel.fr/ ! - Julien Tant (AoSix)

Keep up the great work Dayle! A wonderful resource. Thank you to the @laravel team. @taylorotwell you are really changing the php world. - Douglas Grubba

Thanks Doug! I'm sure Taylor will also be pleased to hear that he is changing the PHP world, one method at a time!

With Laravel I think what I want and not how to write it. I enjoy programming. (Con Laravel pienso quÃ© es lo que quiero y no como escribirlo. Me divierto programando.) - Enrique Lopez

Thanks also to Phill Sparks, who paid the most for the title but never got round to giving a quote. I hope this works for you buddy!

---

[1]http://www.helpspot.com/

24.2 Payments over $9.99

- Andrew Smith
- Proger_XP
- Max Schwanekamp
- Kim Botticelli
- Mike Jones
- Marc Carson
- David Wosnitza AKA _druuuuuuuu
- Mark van der Waarde from Alsjeblaft!
- Joseph Wynn
- Dave Berry
- Shawn McCool
- Alexander Karisson
- Victor Petrov
- Josh Kennedy
- Alexandru Bucur
- William Manley
- Nate Nolting
- Jorijn Schrijvershof
- Caleb Griffin
- Florian Uhlrich
- Stefano Giordano
- Simon Edwards
- Olivier Gaudin
- Vladimir Kapustin
- Tomasz Tomczyk
- George Drakakis

- Michael Dimitriadis

- David Murray

I'd also like to say thanks to everyone that sent kind emails about the book, thanks for all the support!